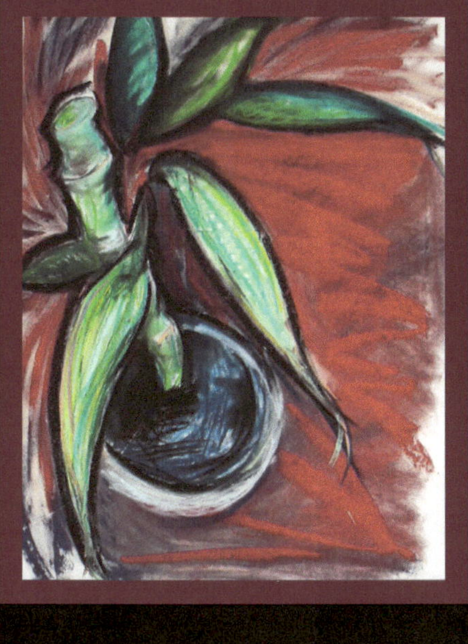

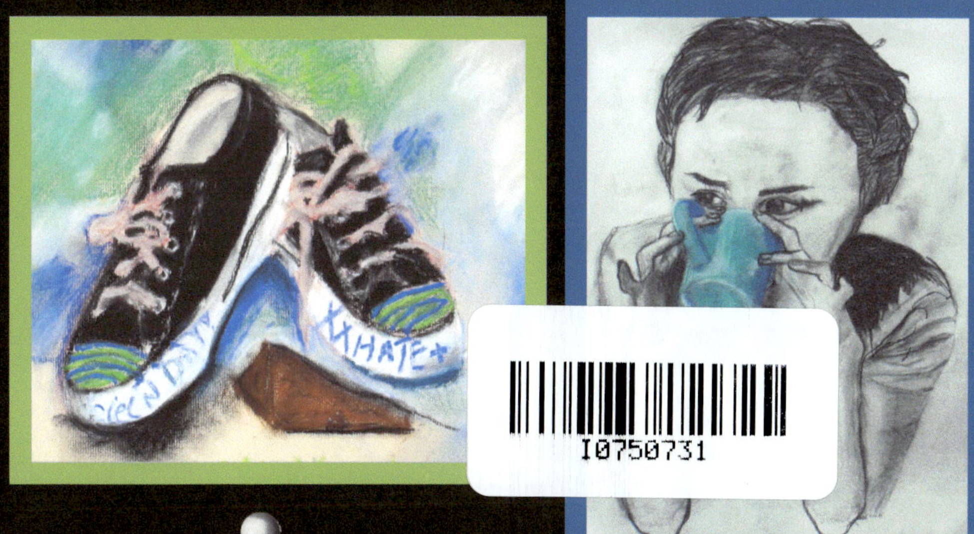
I0750731

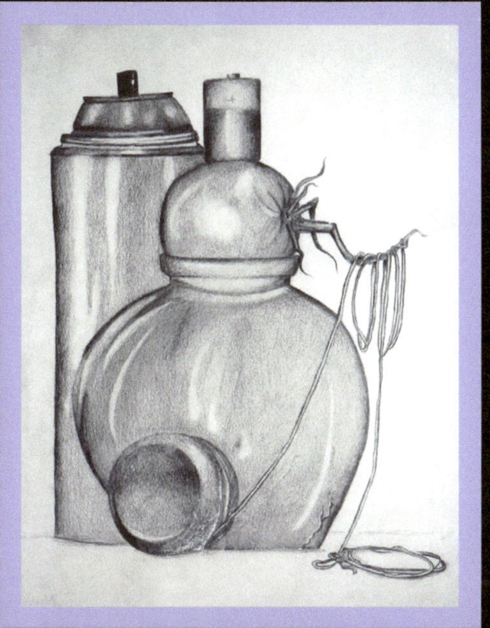

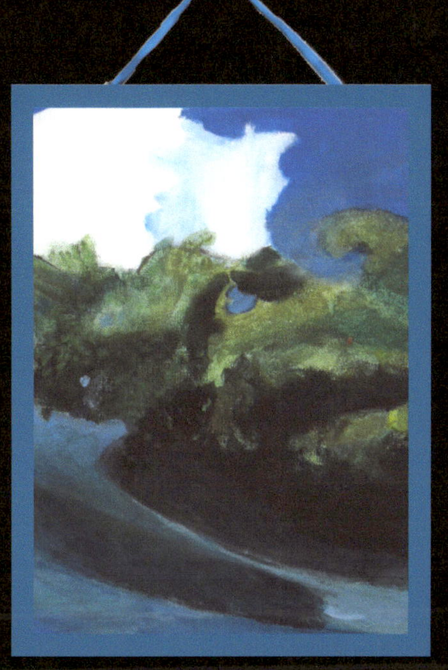

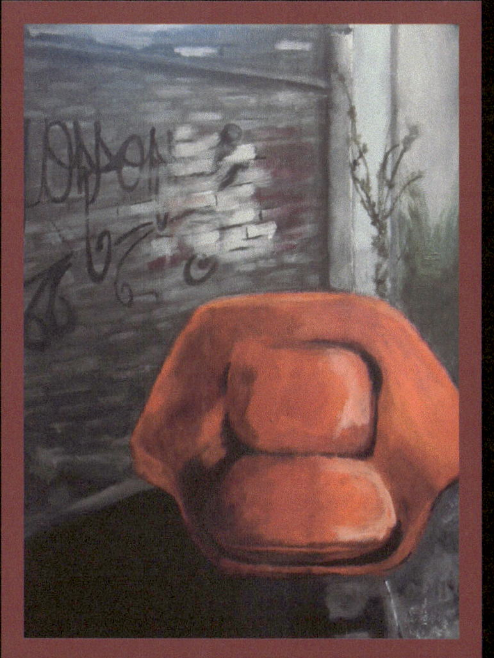

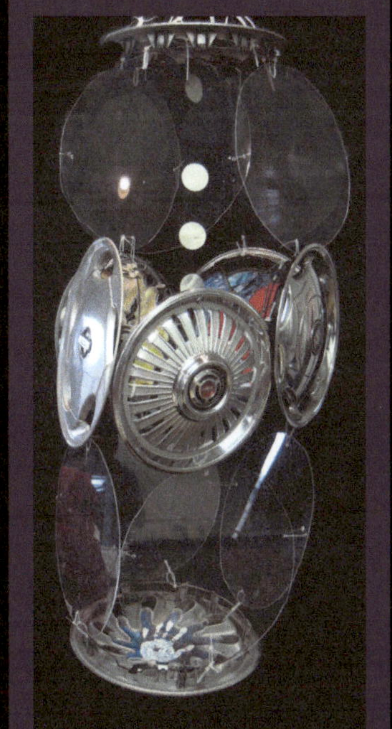

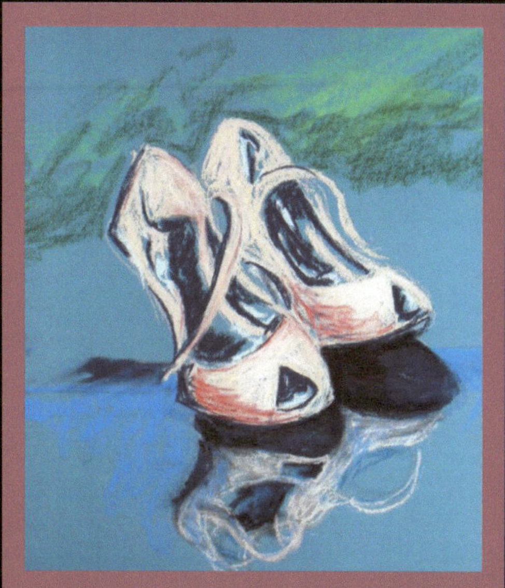

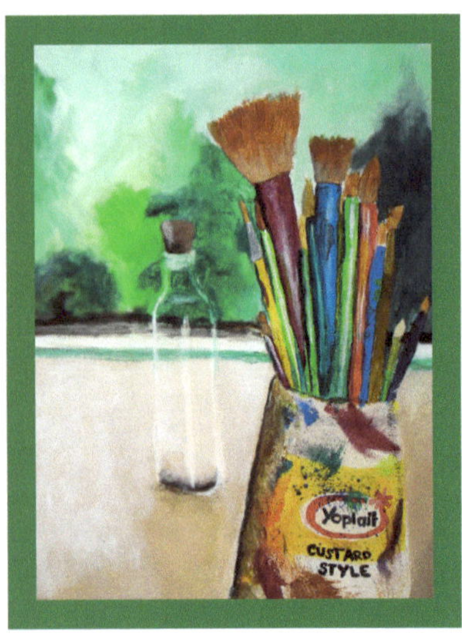
Yoplait
CUSTARD STYLE

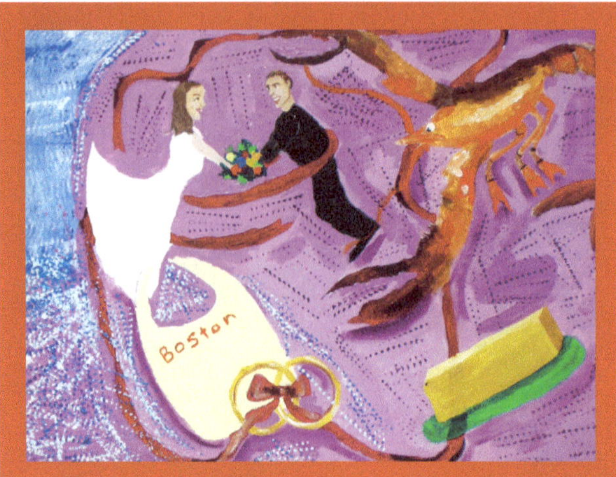
Boston

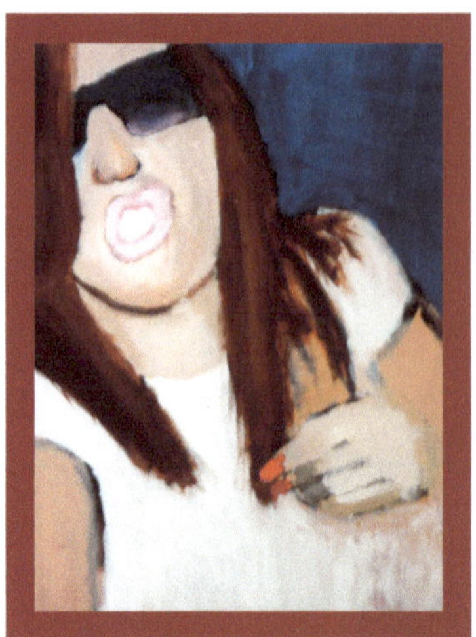

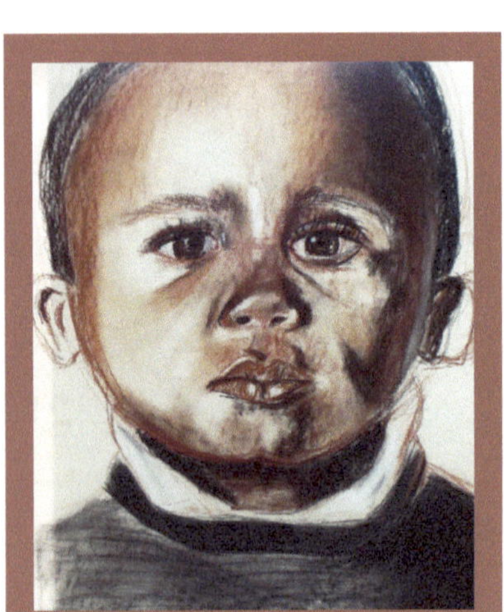

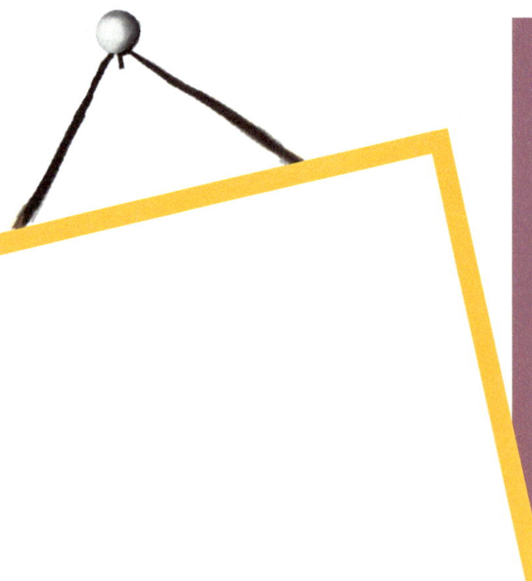
Your Art Here

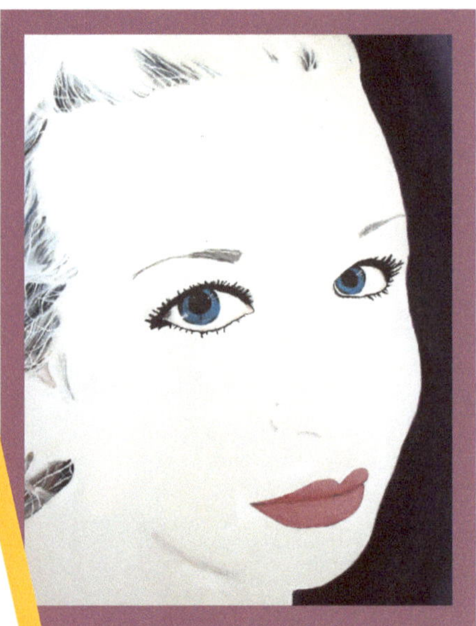

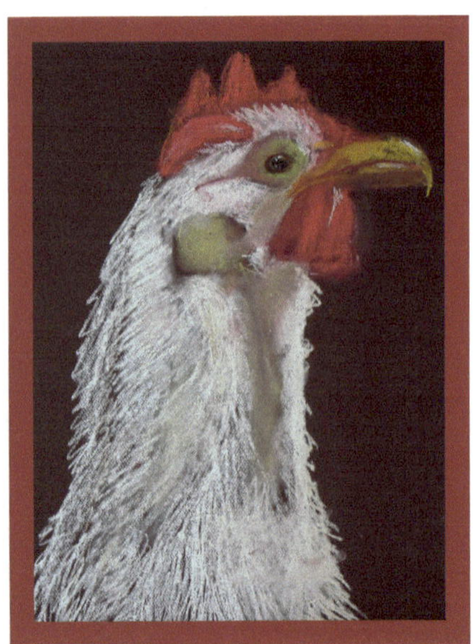

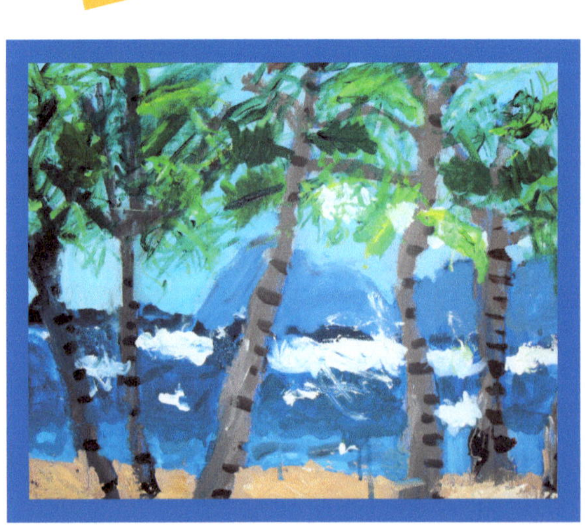

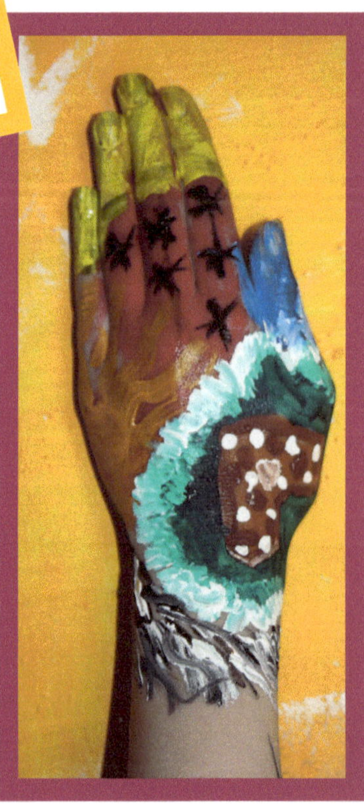

Portrait of a Girl And Her Art

by Elena Caravela

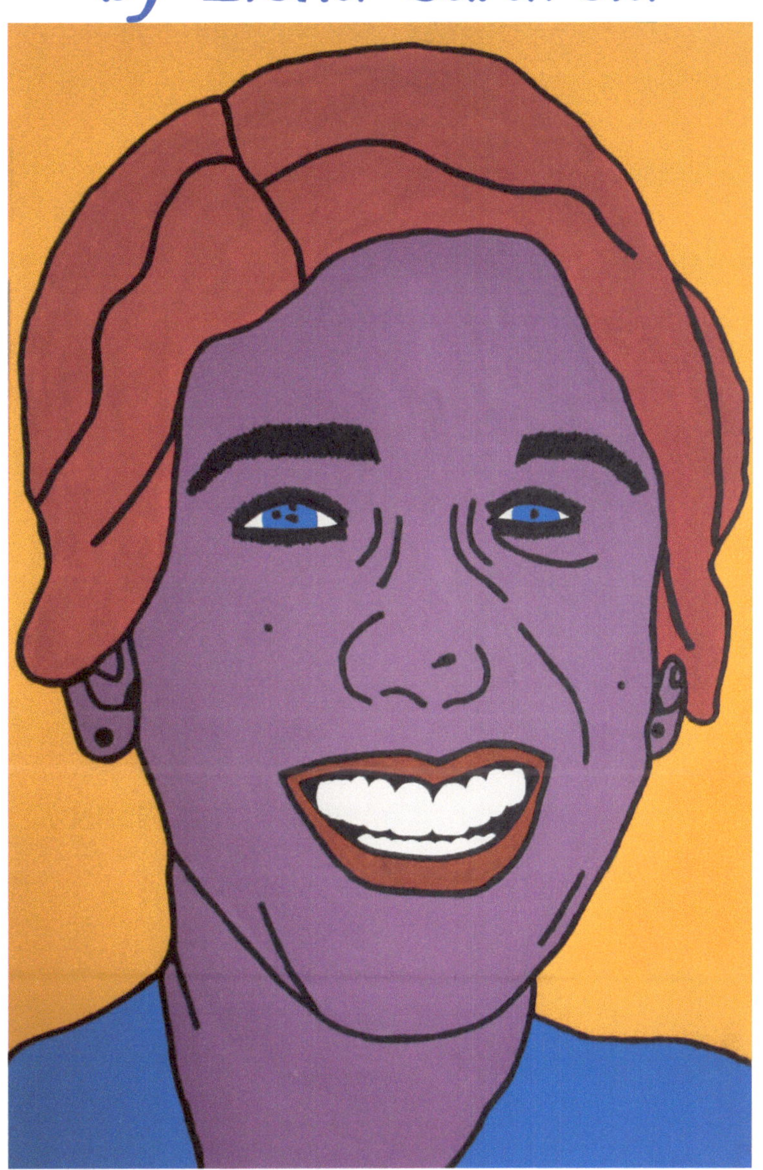

"Elena" by Katie

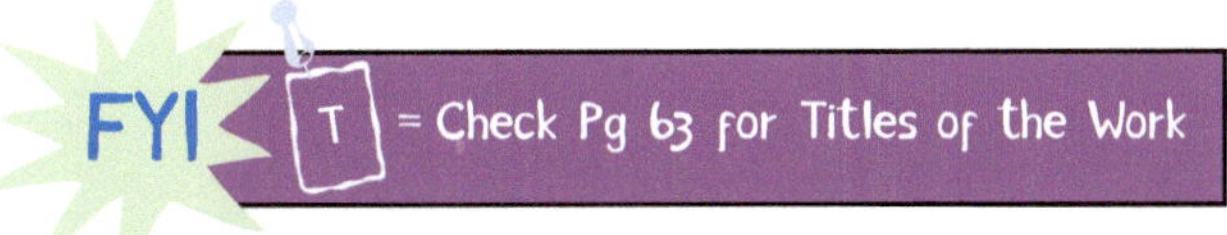

If you are interested in learning more about any of the artists or artwork within this book, please visit the "Portrait of a Girl" blog at www.PortraitOfAGirlAndHerArt.wordpress.com or contact Elena Caravela at elena.kidsart@gmail.com.

ISBN 978-0-578-08965-2

Typeset in Intuitive, Lucida Sans, & Pecita.

Cover Designed by Elena Caravela & Leah Olbrich.

Copies available at Amazon.com, BarnesAndNoble.com, & Lulu.com and through Baker & Taylor.

To all young artists. Believe.

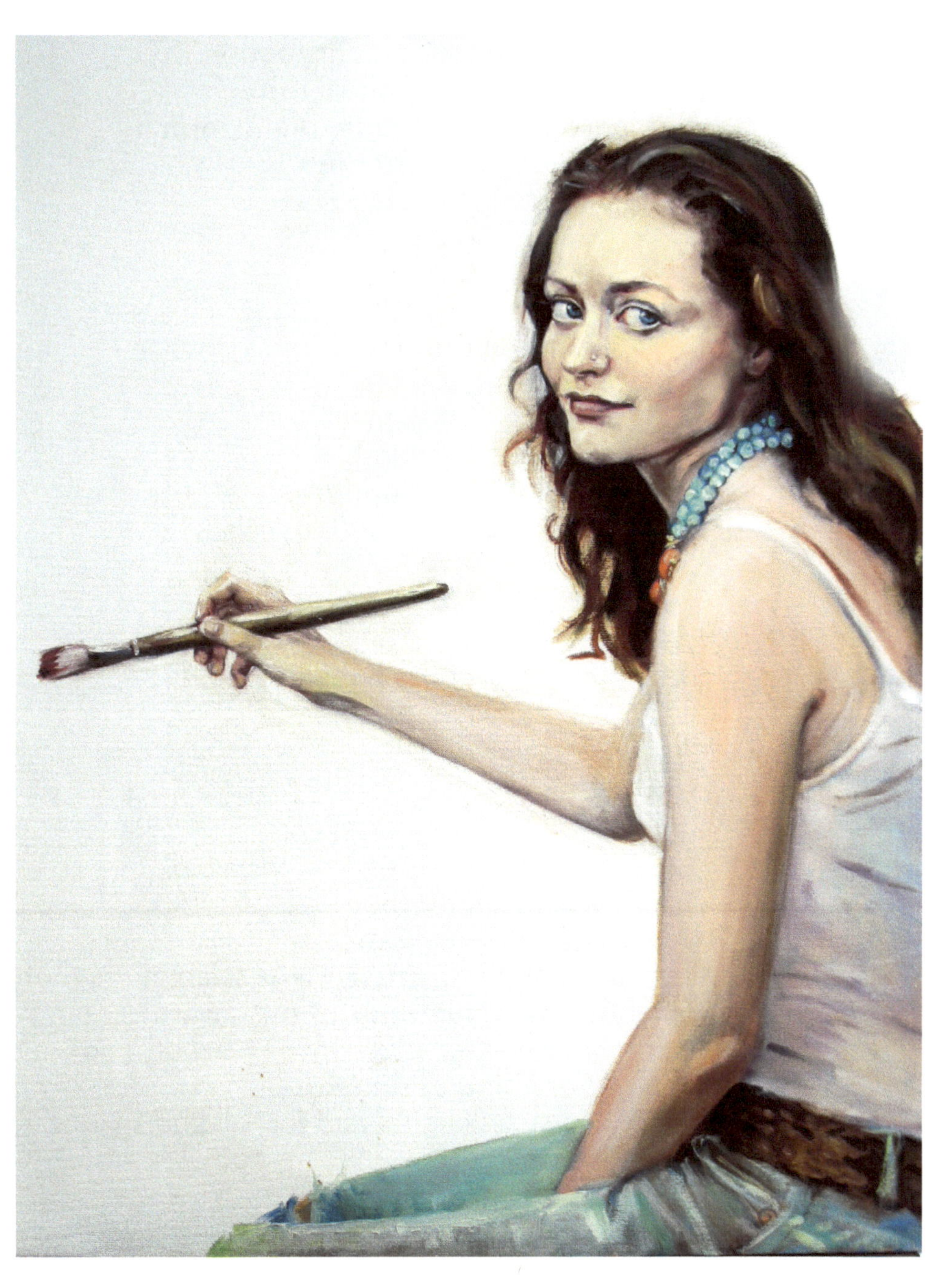

Acknowledgments:

All of these important people
helped in more ways than
I am able to specify. I would like to thank
them all heartily for EVERYTHING.
Many thanks to;
Jack Caravela, for writing, editing
Leah Olbrich, design, layout, research, editing, writing, insightful assistance
Elizabeth Lapinsky, design, layout
Thomas Cartwright, support, design contribution
Julian Cartwright, design contribution
Vaughn Cartwright, contributor
Mary Watson, portrait photos, title, brainstorming
The Triangle of Strength
Marie Caravela
Pam McKelvey
Elaine Murdock
Katie Murdock
Sharon Church
Angela Coleman
Dr. Sudesh Jain
Nancy Lockwood
My family who continue to support my efforts
All of the awesome contributing artists
&
All of the parents who
helped me gather materials, allowing
this book to become a reality.

About the Author

An instructor, illustrator, and fine artist, Elena is an alumna of The School of Visual Arts and illustrator of two award winning children's picture books, *The Birds of the Harbor*, and *A Night of Tamales and Roses.*
"My world is a wonder of visual delights and foreboding shadowy shapes, vying every waking moment for my full attention."

See more from Elena at:
www.ElenaCaravela.net

Introduction: How This Book Came to Be

Creating art has been my refuge, a place where I have always found joy and solace. Throughout the challenges in my life, great and small, making art has forged my identity and has become my saving grace.

And as I approached my fiftieth birthday, I reflected on my life as an artist. Besides creating my own work, I have been teaching art classes and workshops for over twenty years. During that time, I have been privileged to work with many talented young artists, all of whom share my passion for making art. There is, however, a special kinship that I share with young female artists. I remember myself at their ages and vividly recall the challenges I faced at each milestone of life and later as an emerging female artist. If I had only known when I was a girl, that the act of making art would serve me as faithfully as it has throughout my life, I would have been gratefully reassured. This realization sparked the plan for this book. My intention is to share experience, to instill confidence, and inspire creativity in young women as they grow as women and artists.

I began my book by creating a series of traditional portraits of a few of my students. On 30'' x 40'' canvases I incorporated, with respect, images from each student's artwork into the background of my oil portraits. My hope is to present the viewer not only with a likeness of each artist, but also a glimpse into her world through her art.

Next I compiled the text for the book from a questionnaire I prepared for the girls. I asked, "If you had a younger sister, what would you tell her about how you begin your creative process? About how you choose your ideas, subject matter, and medium? And most importantly, how has the process of creating art affected you?" Then I realized that I needed to expand my vision to include girls that I did not already know. Family and friends of friends assisted me in recruiting more young female visual artists from around the country. I learned about them through painting their portraits, reviewing their quotes and enjoying their artwork. Since the young women surveyed varied from age six to twenty, the answers to my questions were very different. But a common theme in all of the answers reflected the healing, joyful, insightful, and confidence-building effects art can offer a young woman.

In "Portrait of a Girl" I have showcased fifteen young artists. Alongside their portraits, you will find quotes from each artist. In addition, many more girls inspired by the fifteen featured added their art to the book. At the end of each chapter is a section entitled "Your Way," a guide of sorts, for drawing inspiration from each artist's point of view.

For me, this book is a celebration of being an artist. It has taken me five years to complete. During that time, all of the young artists have grown in many ways. Some have pursued careers in visual art while others effectively incorporate their artistic expressions into their daily lives. In every case creating art has been quite valuable in obvious and unexpected ways. All of the young artists in this book continue to awe and inspire me. I thank them not only for their contributions to my book, but for their sincerity and enthusiasm. I couldn't be more proud to introduce them all to you.

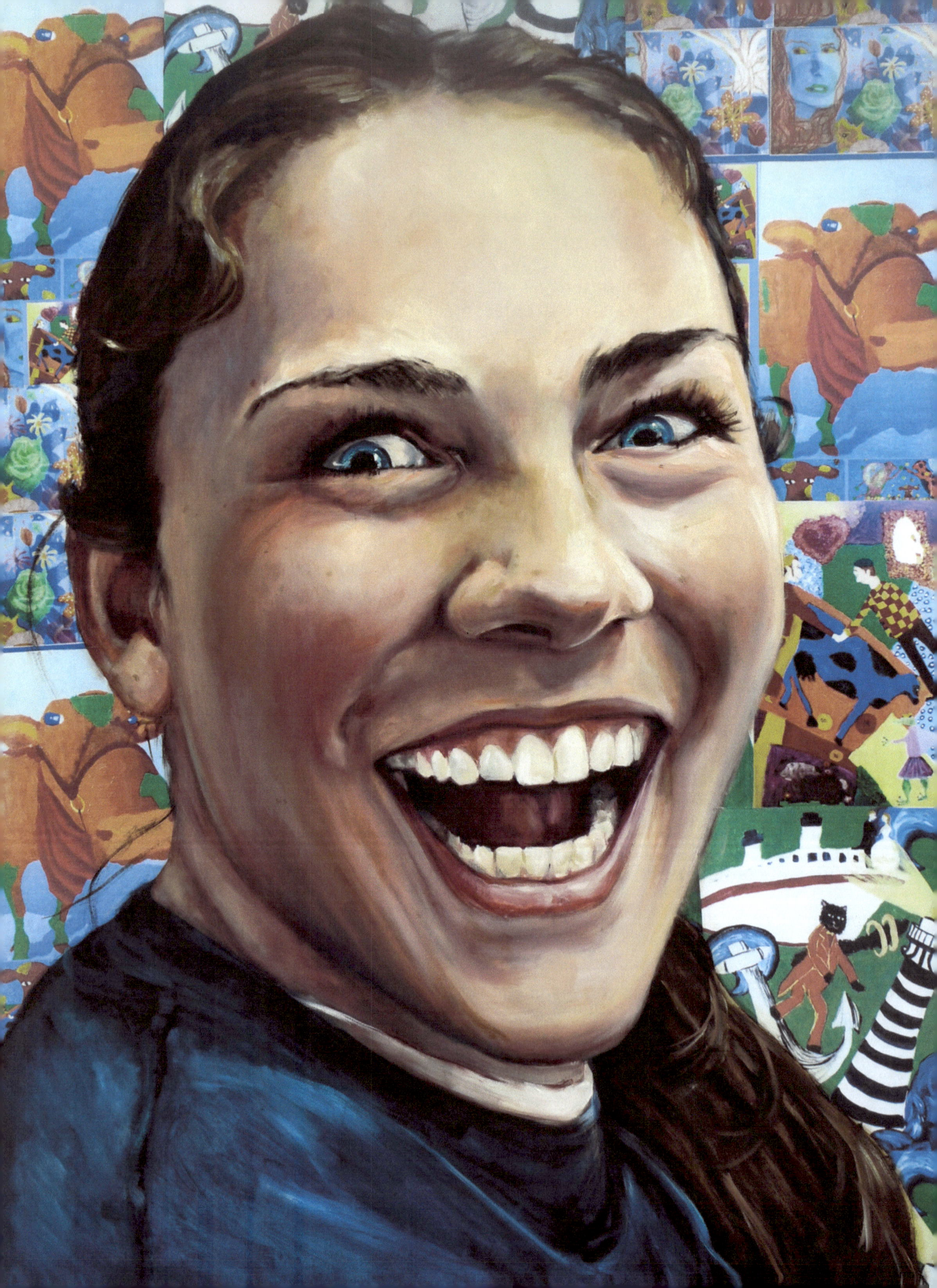

My World

I remember the feeling of joy I experienced when I finished my senior art collection. I created seventeen portraits of my family and friends. I loved every one of them. They all seem to be full of so much energy and light.

When I finish a piece it feels like I have just given birth to a baby!

-Katie

These four panels show us what Katie was feeling on September 11, 2001, interpreting events through her eyes as she worried whether her father would return home safely. On the following page is another piece by Katie, entitled "My Cousin's Wedding." In it, Katie selected a few of the things she remembered best about the couple, including a cruise ship and a cat, set in a whirlwind of joyous color.

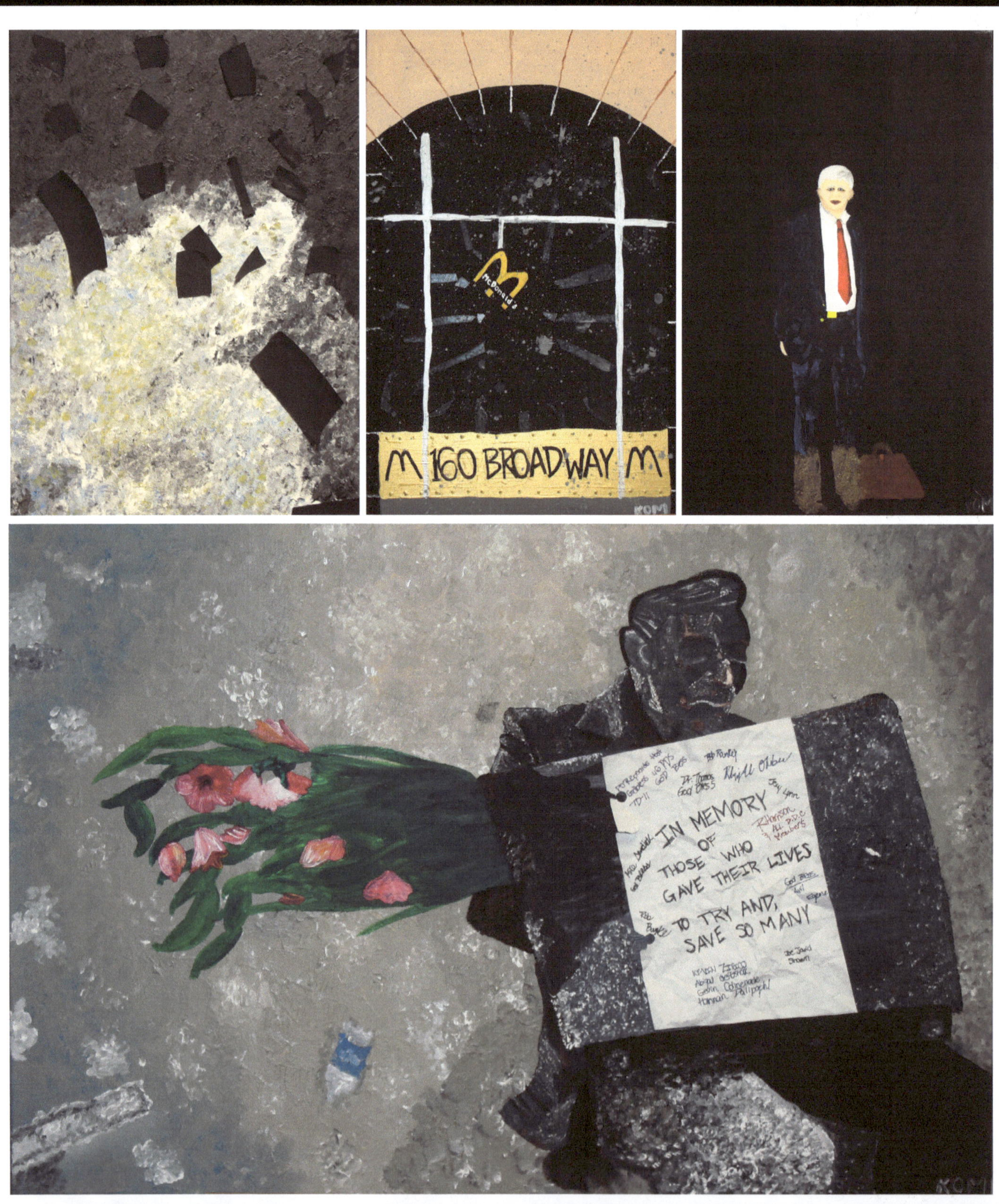

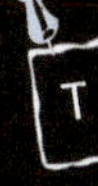

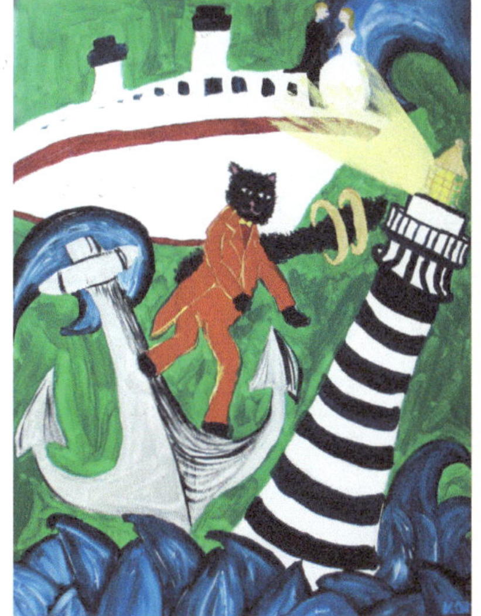

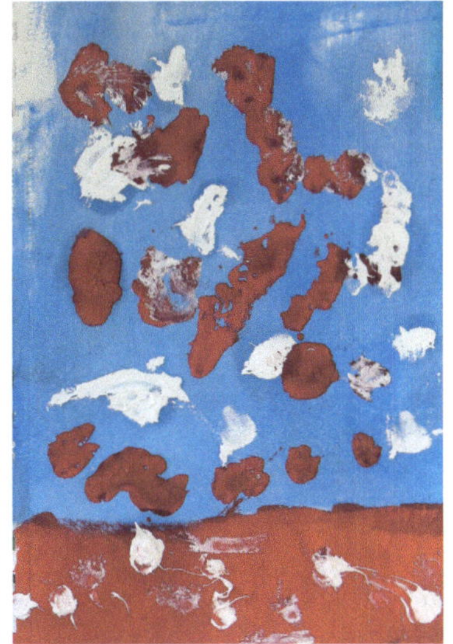

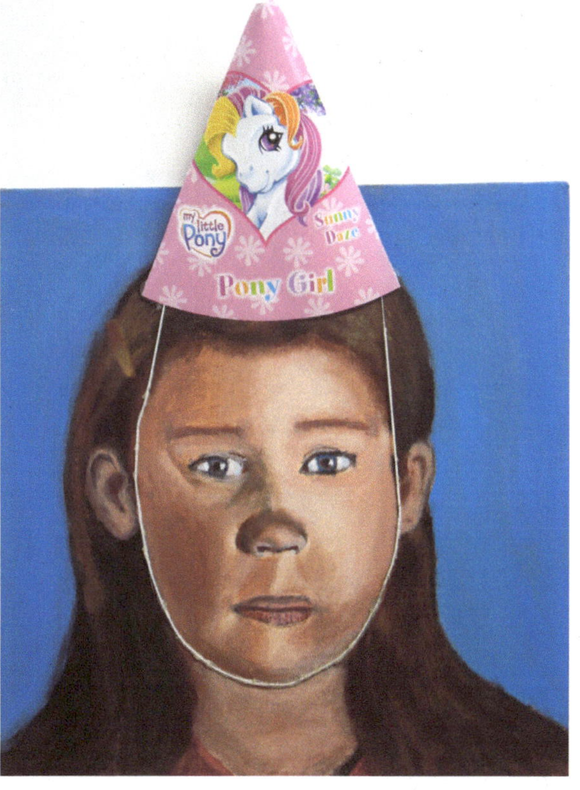

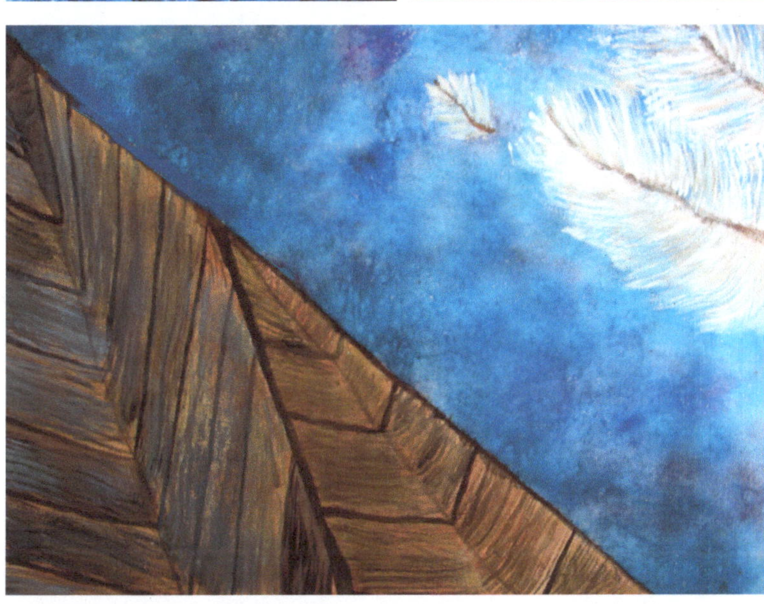

Your Way

How do you feel about the events that are shaping your world? Is there a particular event that immediately comes to mind? Many events influence your everyday life. Look for ideas among your recent photographs or family calendar or from headlines in current newspapers or magazines. Ask yourself questions about why and how this affects you. Once you have chosen an event that you sincerely care about, present the thing that is important to you. Give it a visual voice.

About Katie pg 64

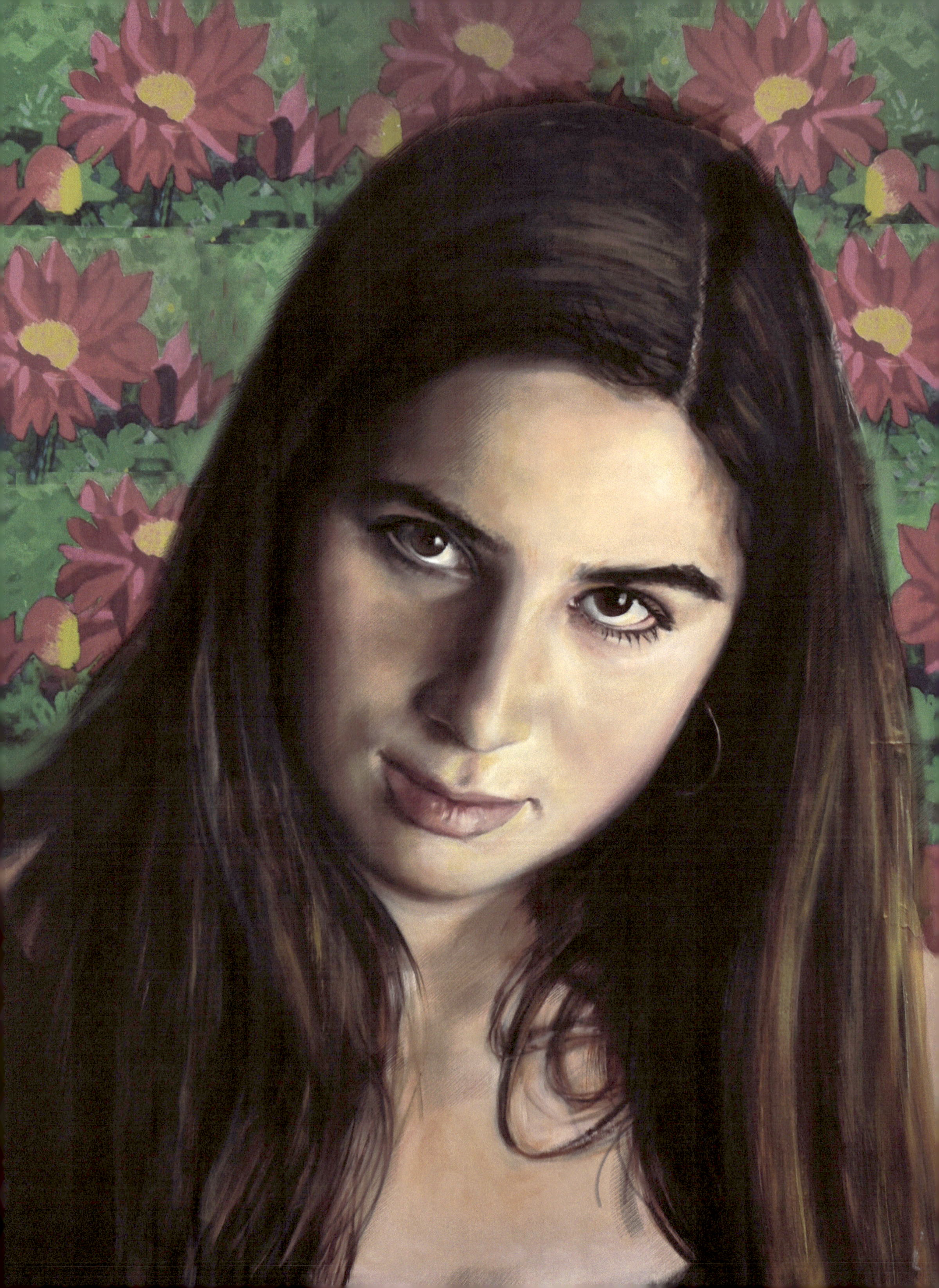

Multipurpose

I started doing art when I was little. I remember I was three years old when I began to draw. I drew some colorful and beautiful drawings using markers, paint, pencils and crayons. My artwork became like real life, because my art was about things that happened to me every day.

You can make paintings, beads, and pencils work. You can do just about anything.

I feel so proud when people like my art. It makes me feel happy and relaxed. I'm having a good time.

-Lara

Like Lara, many artists make crafts (ex. pottery), fine art (ex. paintings or sculptures) and commercial art (ex. graphic art or illustrations). Are these categories really that different? Are they valued in the same way? Is it all art, or does it depend on how you choose to look at it? Objects that have a specific function in our daily lives don't have to BE just one thing. For instance, Lara is an illustrator and fine artist.

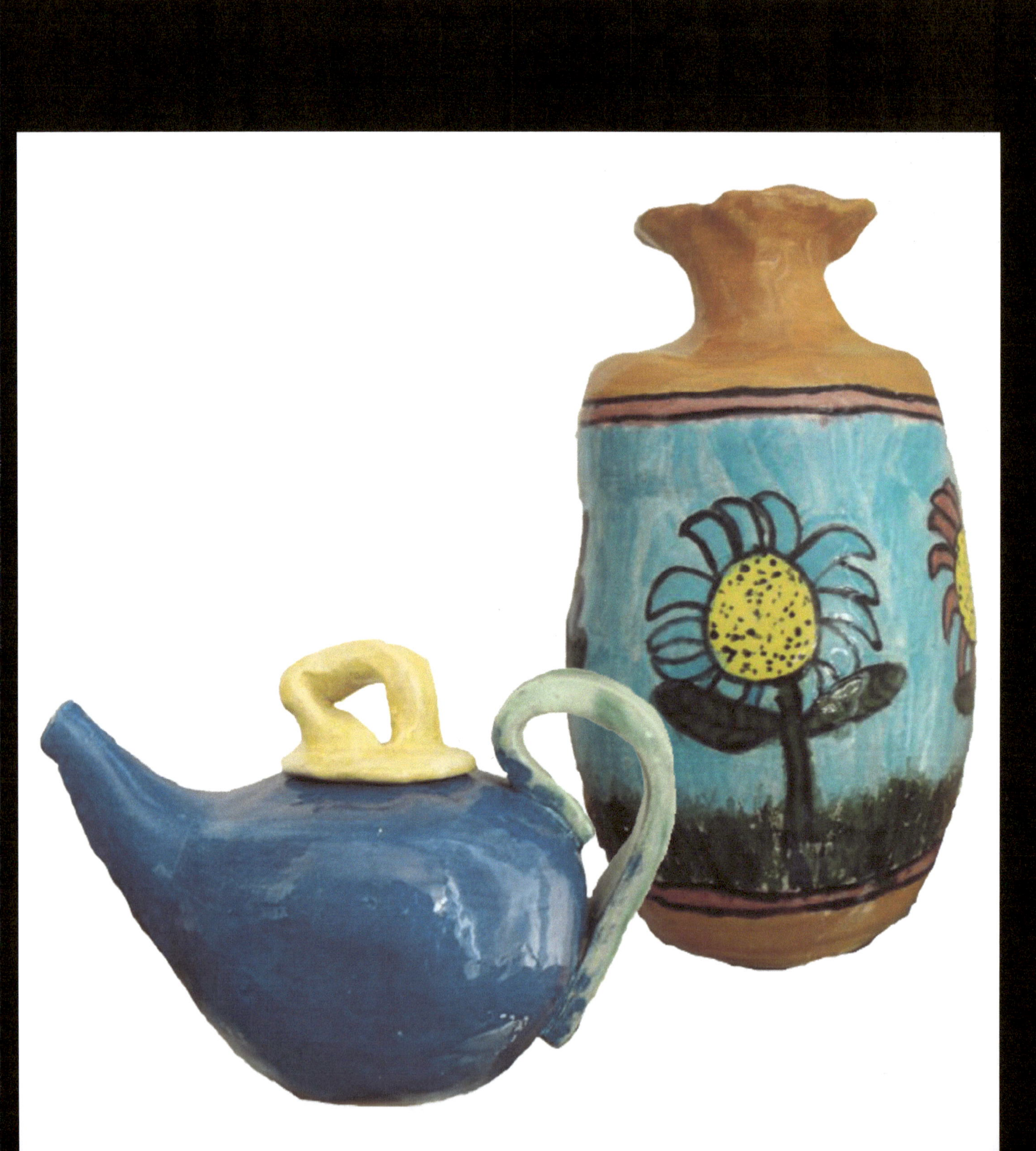

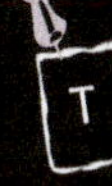

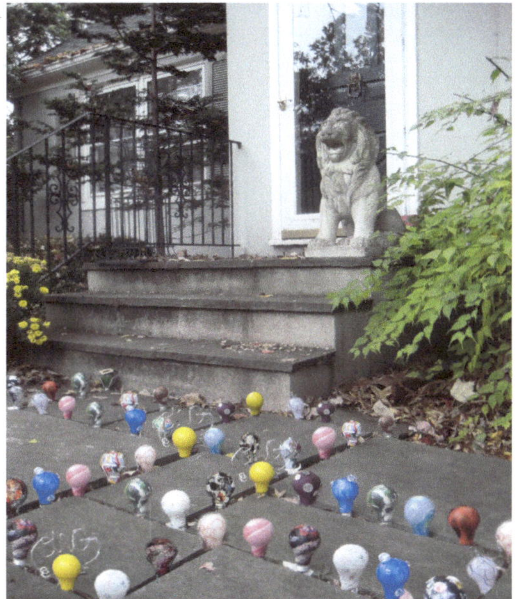

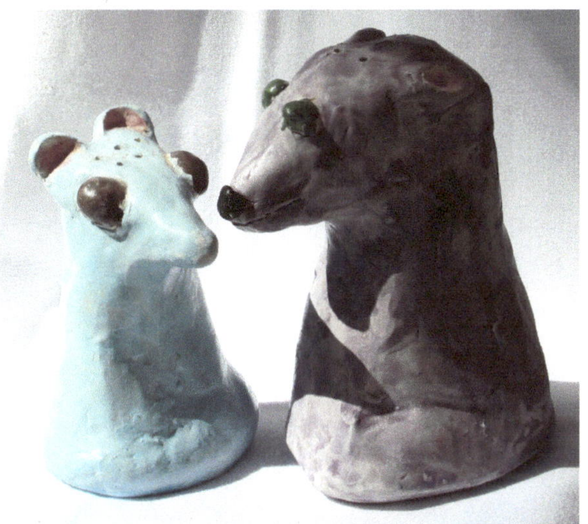

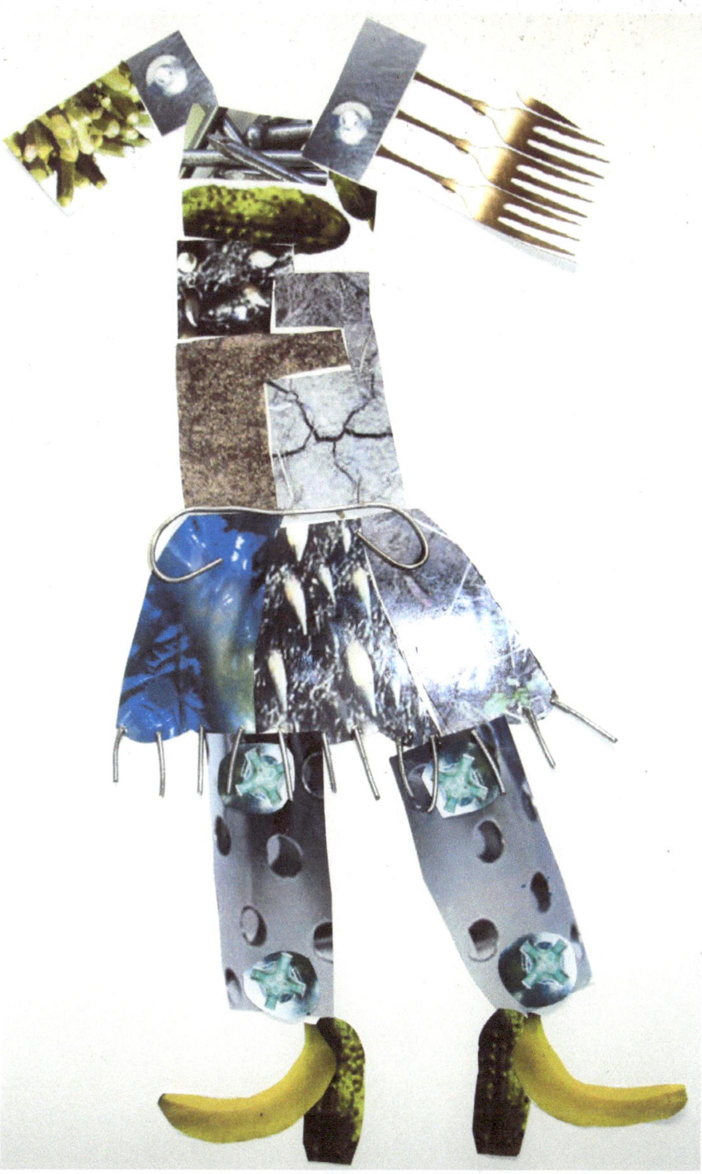

Your Way

Look around your home, focus on various objects, and ask yourself: "Is this an object of art?" If your answer is "no," then consider how you can make it into art. Also ask yourself, "Did someone design this thing"? If your object is something you can modify, add new elements to it. If not, draw, paint, or sculpt your vision. See how Taylor has repurposed old lightbulbs. Look closely at Kate's collage and Martha's salt and pepper shakers. What can you do with an old lampshade?

About Lara pg 64

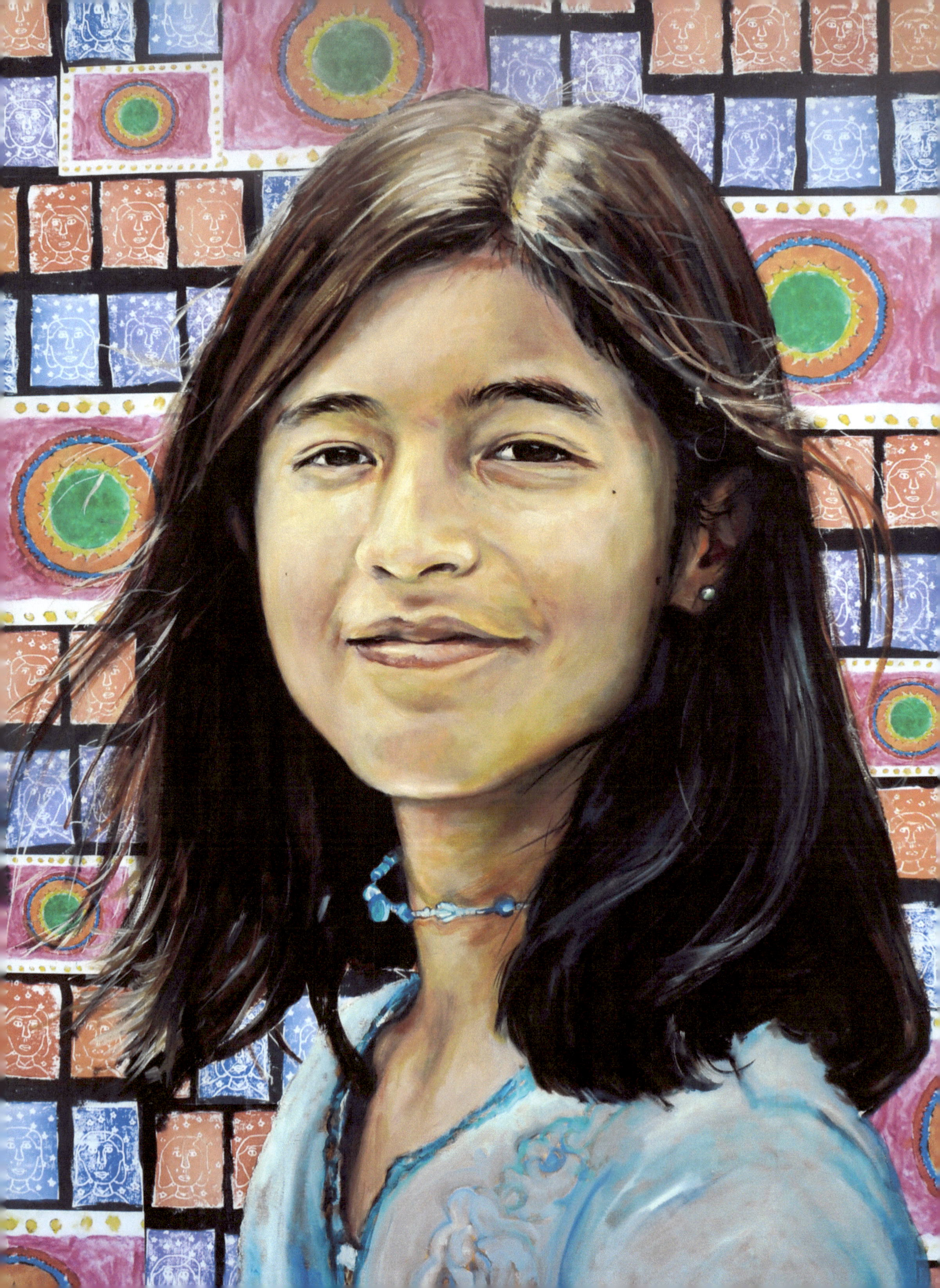

Imagination

In art, nothing can be wrong, it's just how you feel.

Calm and peaceful, yet bold and outgoing, I feel that the color red represents my personality well. It's a happy and cheerful color, but at times sad and angry. Like the color red, through art I can express all these emotions.

-Serena

Serena lets her imagination run free when it comes to visualizing her creations. She uses a structured pattern on her dragon that contrasts with its playful nature. Color and humor allow her work to come alive! In art [and imagination], nothing can be wrong!"

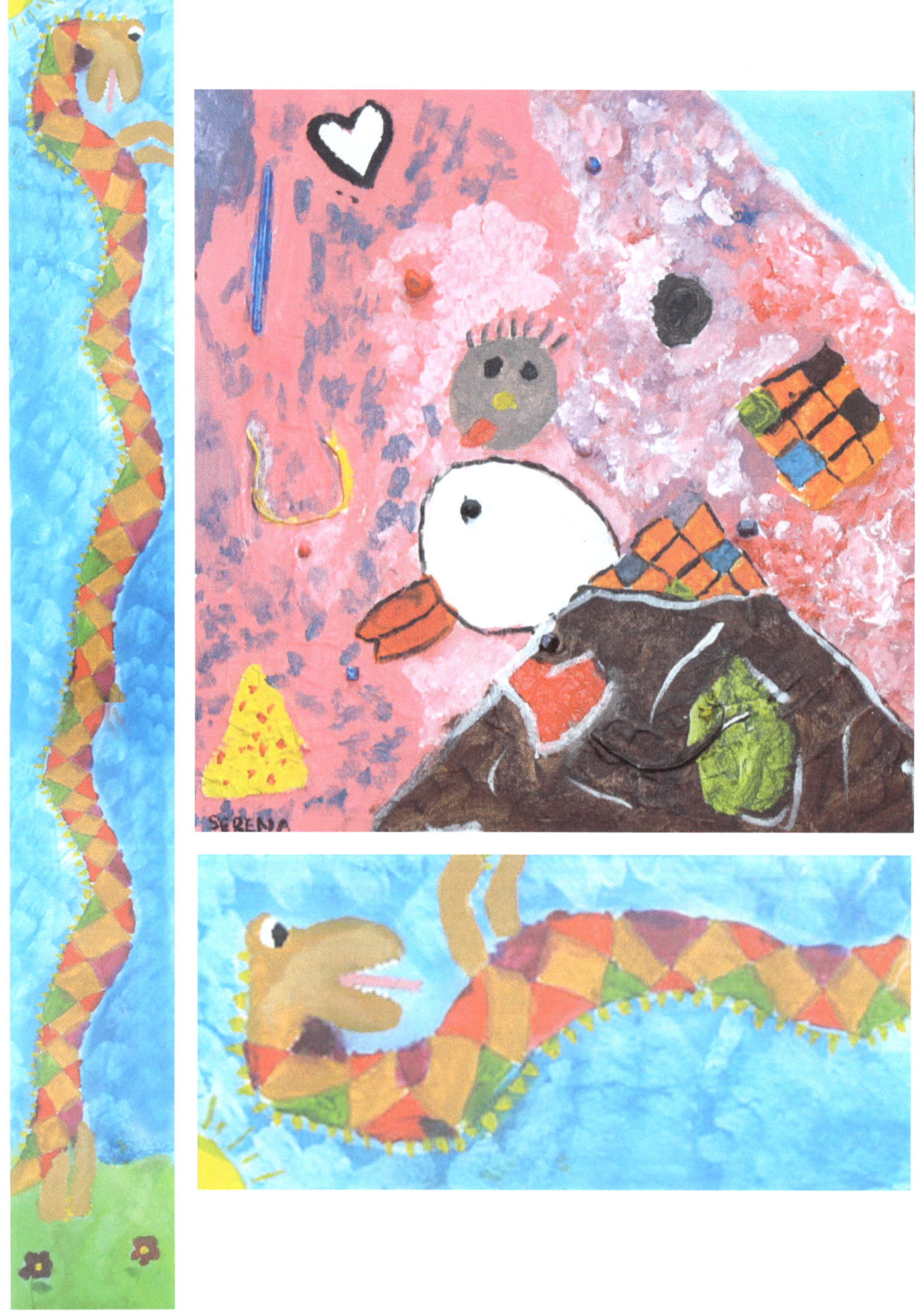

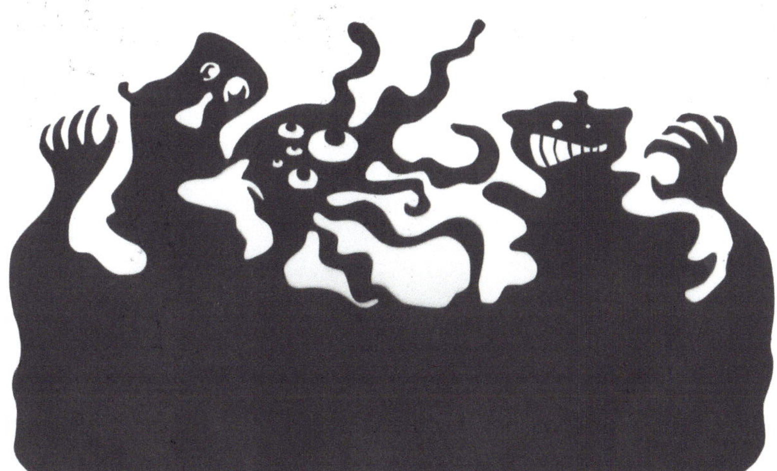

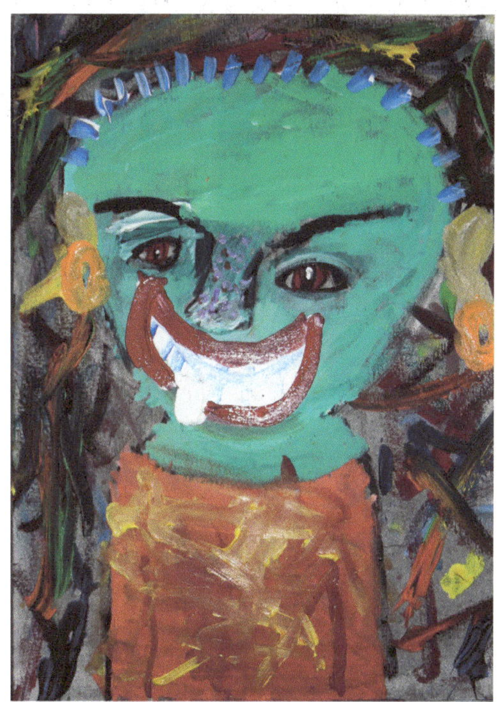

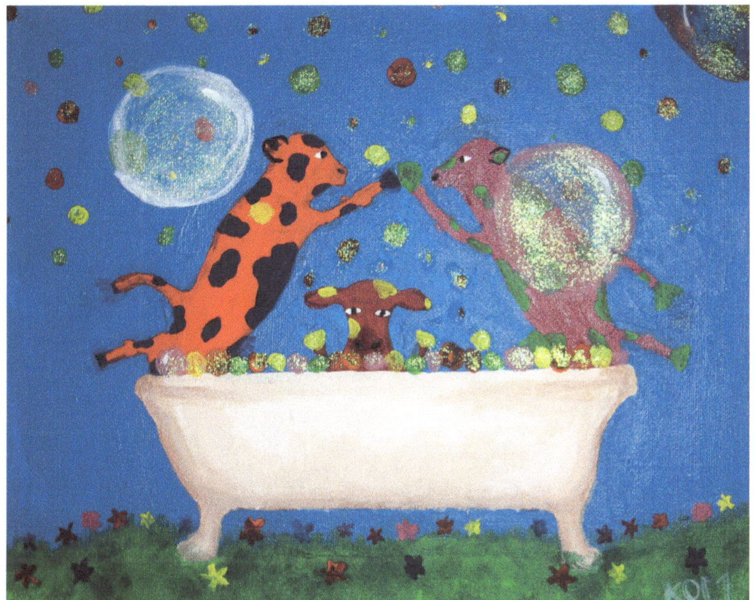

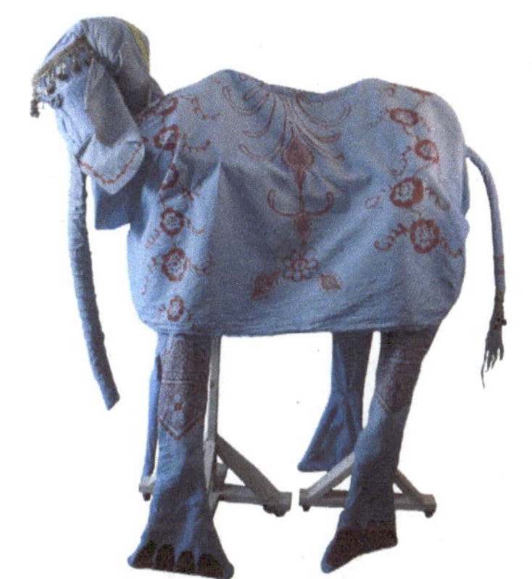

Your Way

Close your eyes and think of a place. Is it a desert? Could it be an ocean? Perhaps it's the inside of a volcano. Then, think about what sort of creature would live in such a place. What would it need to make it happy? Is it a variation on a known creature? Is it a combination of a couple creatures? Is it something completely new? Ask yourself all sorts of questions about your creature. Decide if your fictional friend will be two- or three-dimensional. Then set about making it. Give your creature a name and an imaginary life!

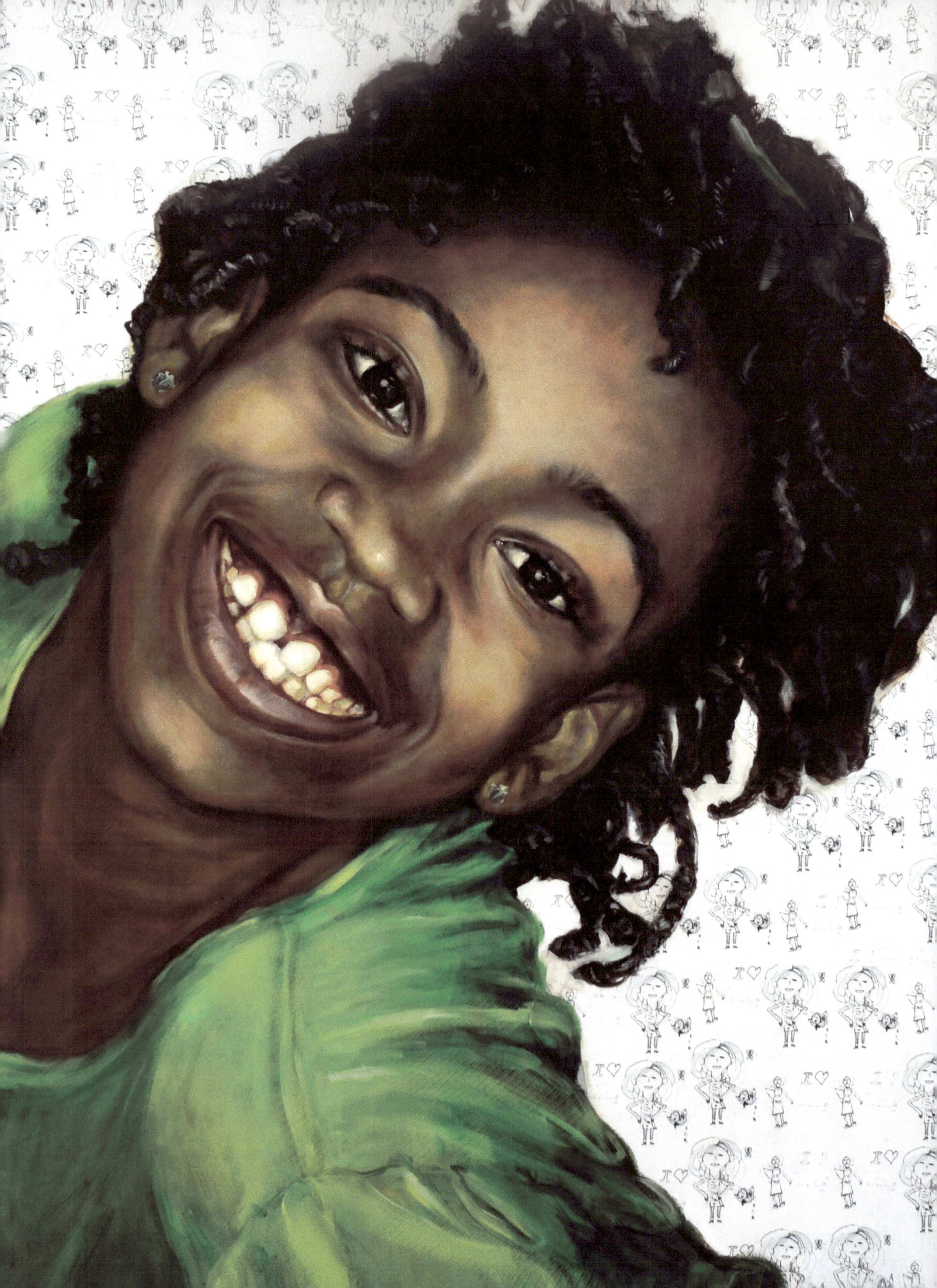

The Artist Inside

"I think of myself as an artist because I was just born with it.

I love to make art because it's fun and you can do whatever you want. I like to draw because it lets my feelings out. I think of my feelings or a thing that happened in my life, and I just put them together to make art.

Art is anything you see and have.

-Ayanna"

Ayanna simply knows that she's an artist. Do you know this too? Artists "see" when they look. Ayanna notices the weave in the wallpaper and the shapes in her rug. Look around your home and "see" it in a new way.

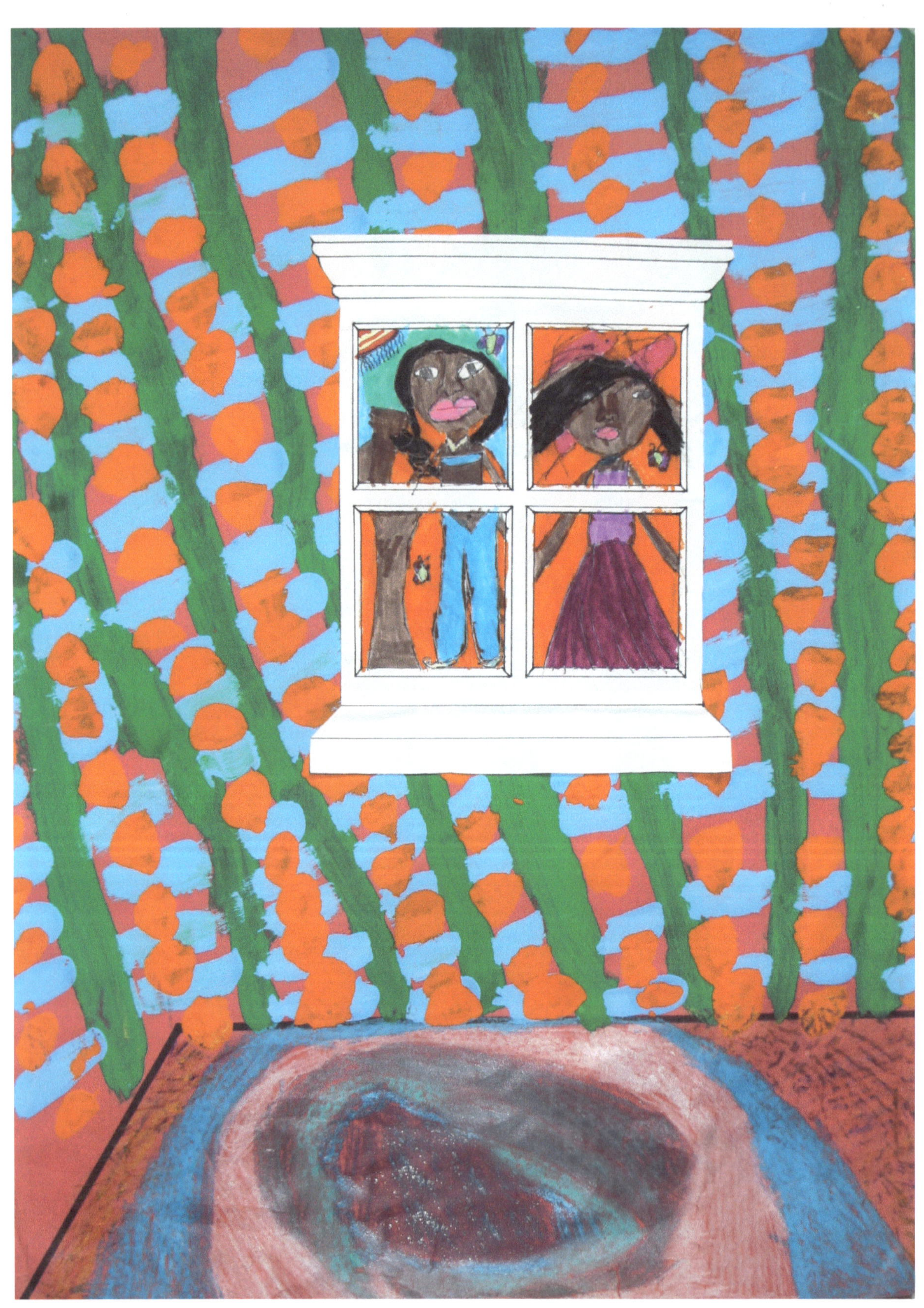

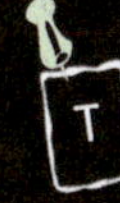

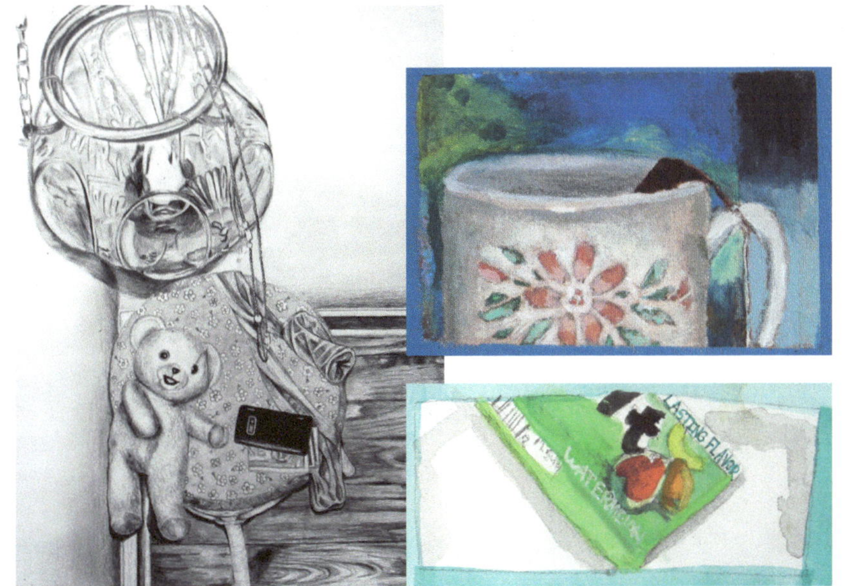

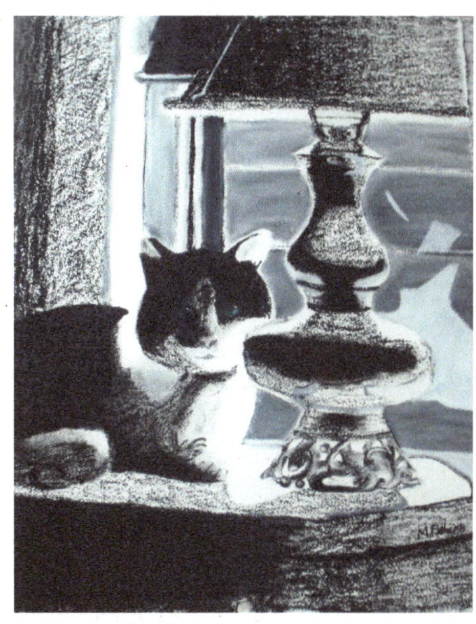

Your Way

Have you ever been frightened by a shadow that turned out to be a hat hanging on a hook or a sweater draped on your dresser? That's just one example of how your perceptions of familiar things can change if you look at them just a little bit differently.

One way to make familiar surroundings look new is to change your point of view. Here are some things to try:

*Lie on the floor and look up at the ceiling.
*Lie on your bed and put your head where your feet usually go.
*Turn objects upside down.
*Use a camera to focus on details and angles of objects, not the entire object.
*Observe your family through a window outside when they don't know that you are watching.
*Find patterns and creatures in wood grains and tiles.
*Look for shadows and the shapes they make.

Set out to "see" more of what is in front of you, or to the side, or to the other side, or in back of you. Inspiration can come from the most familiar places. "Art is anything you see and have." The more you look, the more you will see.

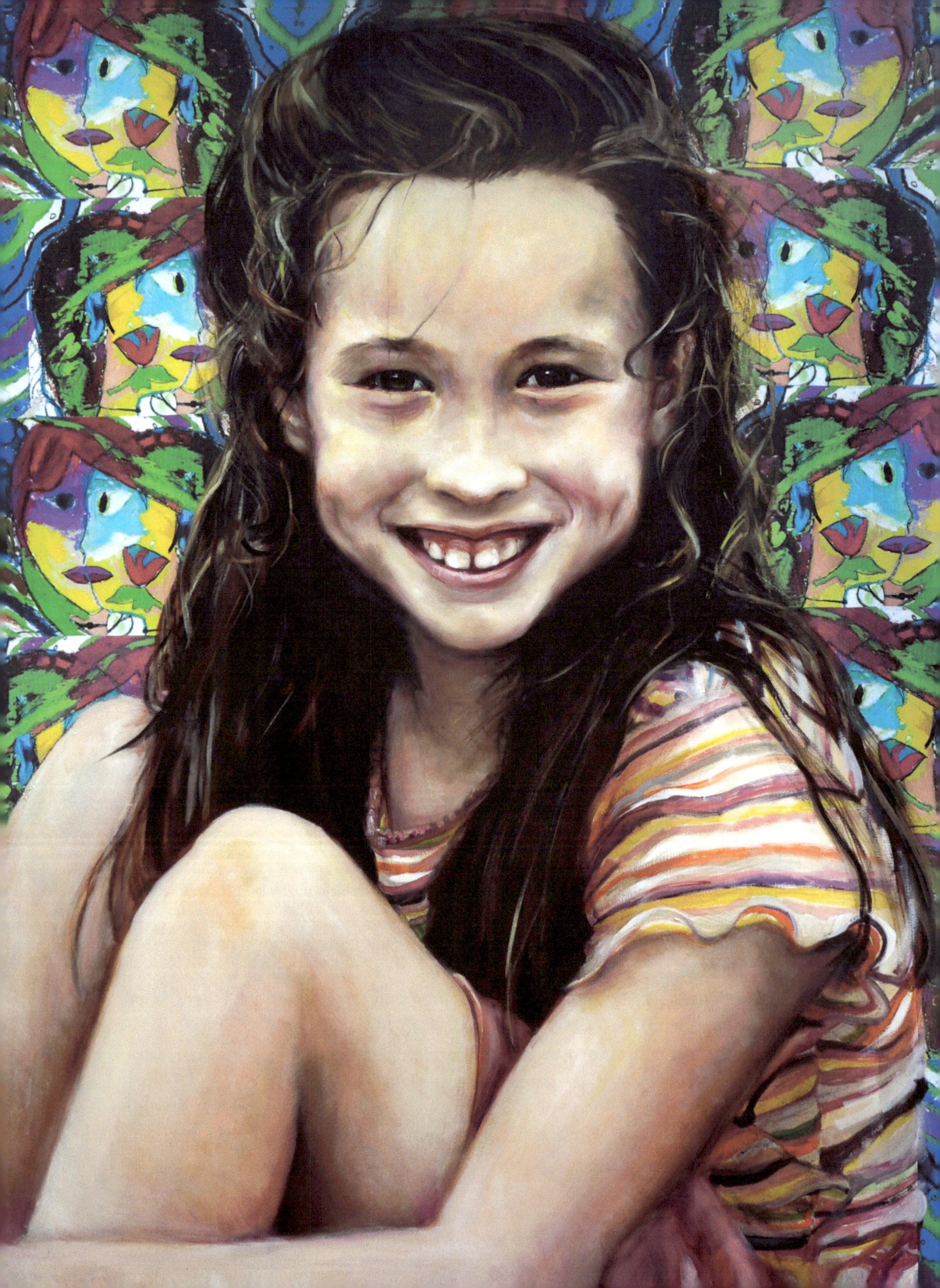

Showcasing

"I was very happy that my artwork was displayed at the Moton Museum. [It] showed a story about how everyone should be equal and get along.

I always think, who wants to go through life unnoticed? I am a good artist, and want people to see my masterpieces.

-Claire"

Not every artist finds support for her work. Sometimes it never happens. Sometimes it happens after many years. But it surely will never happen if an artist is afraid that people will not like her work. Sometimes illustrating themes that you feel require a voice will motivate you to take a chance and make your work public. Claire is showing us a piece with an historical theme. What do you think it's about?

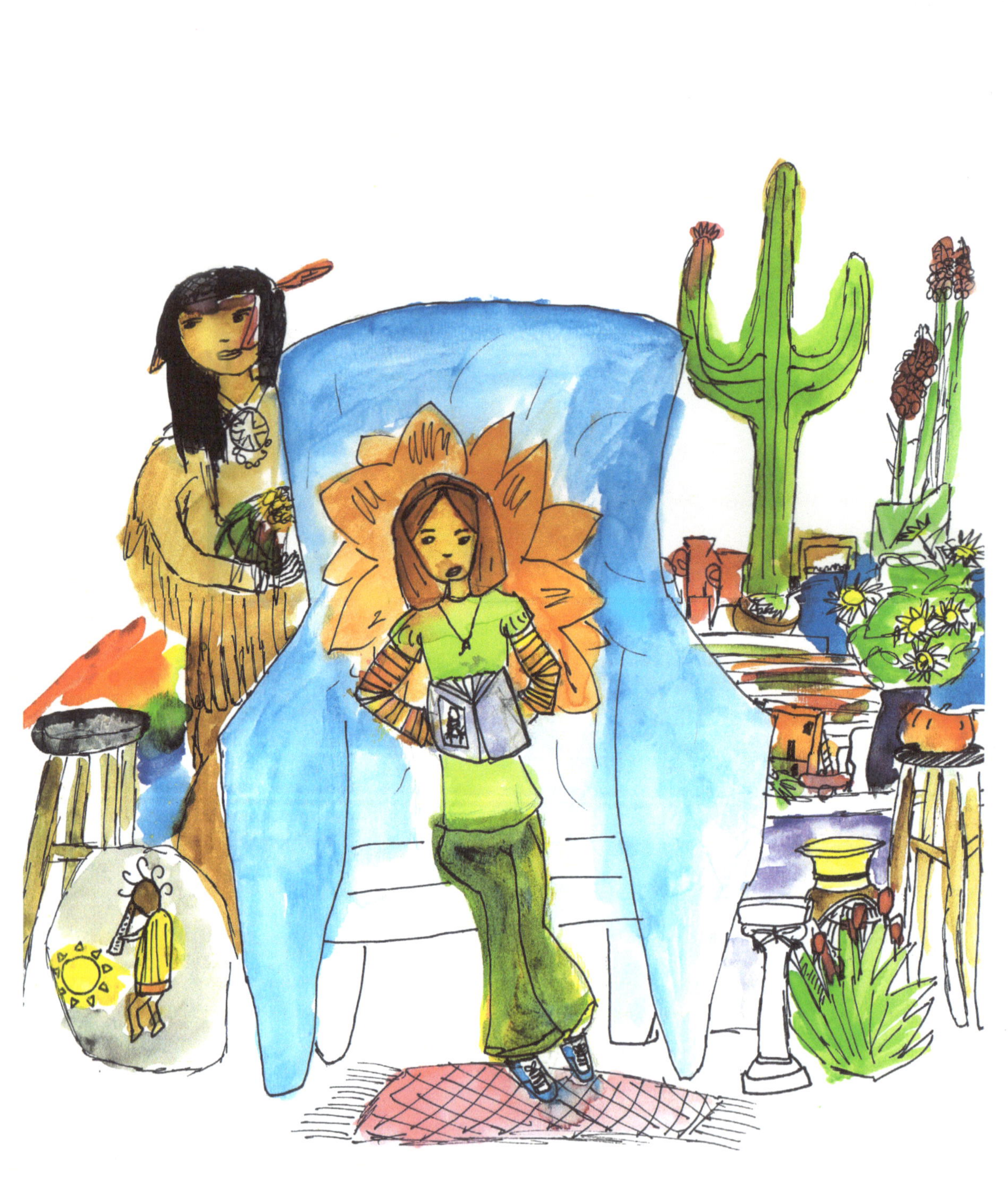

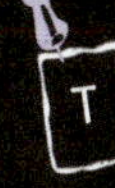

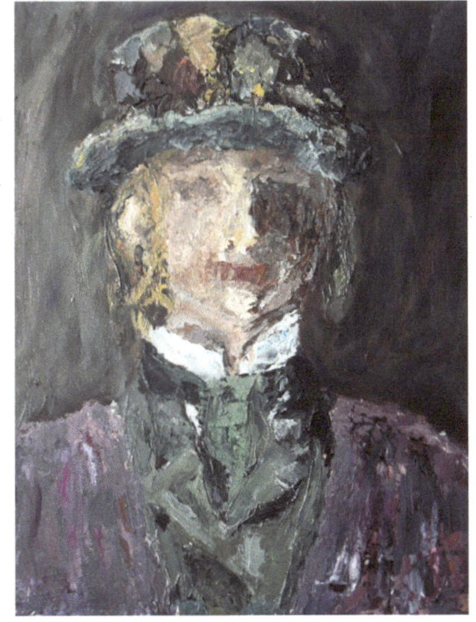

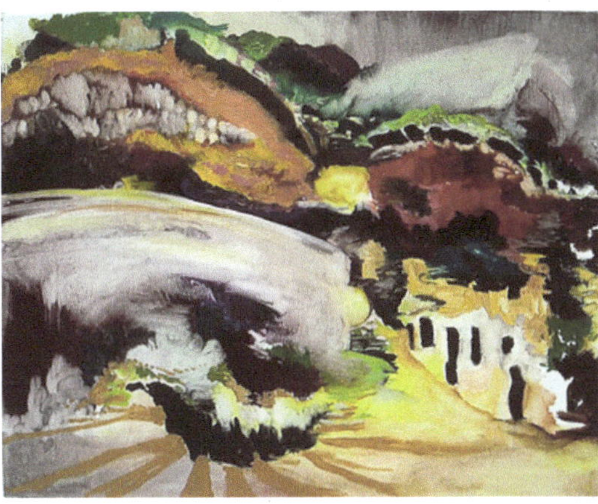

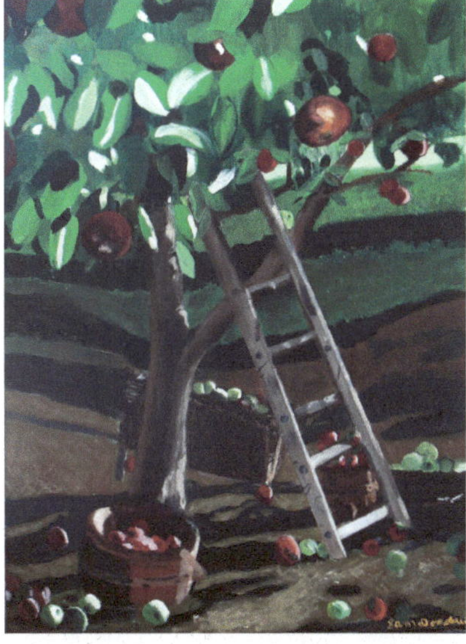

Your Way

Are you shy about showing your art? Do you have a piece that you think needs to be seen? Are you just waiting for an opportunity to show your work?

To start:

Create a place in your home that you can devote to exhibiting your work. The next step may be asking your art teacher to display your piece at school. Look for contests, magazines and websites inviting submissions by young artists. Create your own online space to present your work and share it with family and friends.

You should feel great that you have the confidence to show your work to others. Don't expect everyone to love it—the most important thing is that YOU are proud of your work. If the world likes it too, that's great. Don't be discouraged if it's not an instant hit. Keep working and growing, and continue to bring the work you love into public space.

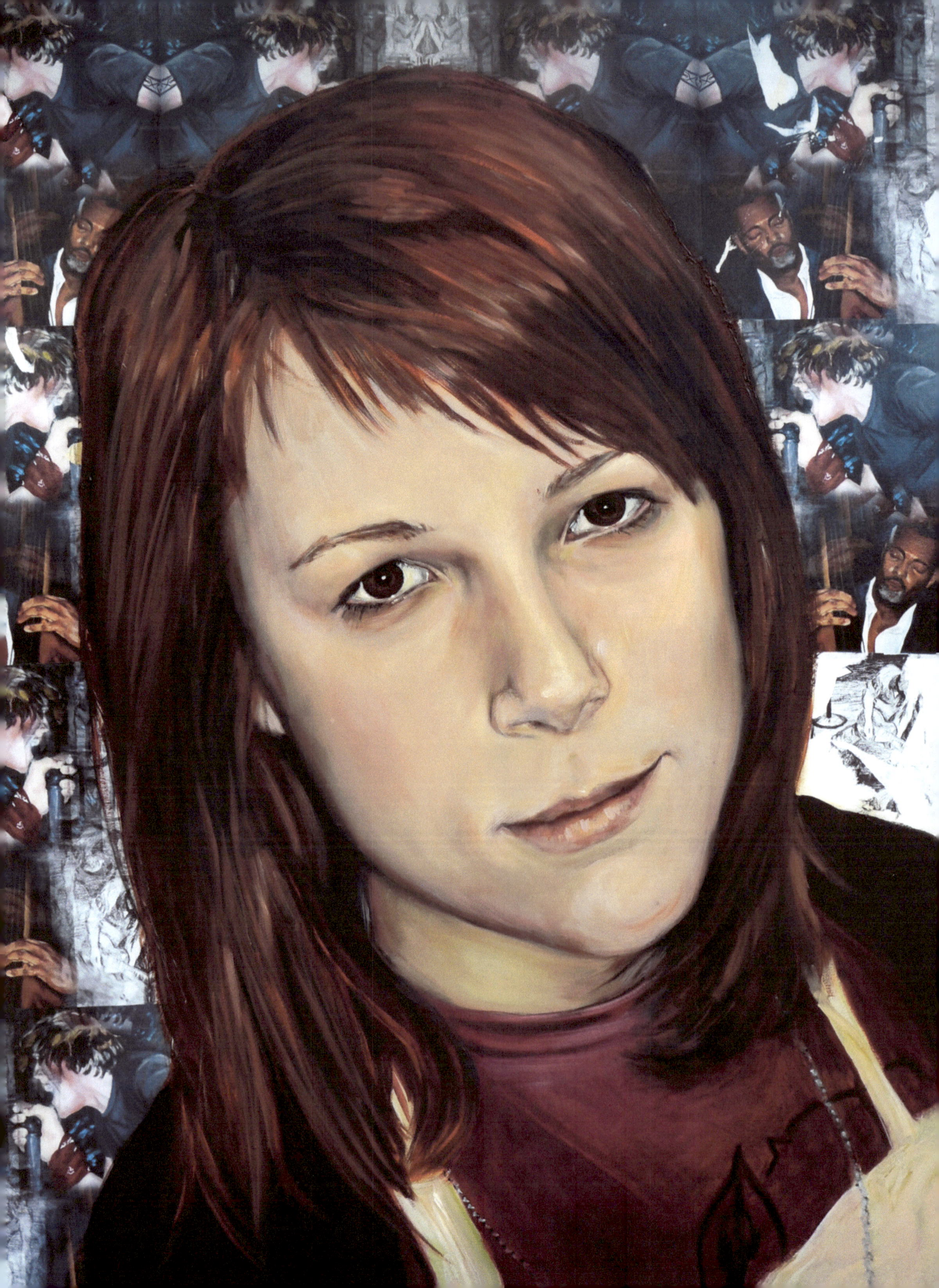

Light and Dark

"To really be comfortable with rendering darks and lights, you need a really good exercise. My professor projected an image on a screen. It was blurred to the point where it was only huge blobs of color. Then about every ten minutes or so, he would rotate the image. We weren't focused on the objects we were painting, just the shapes of the dark and light colors.

Observe and understand the darks first, because they will often better inform your sense of the lights and the values in between.

Oil paints are nice because they are so easy to manipulate, lending themselves to some really exciting effects.

-Cynthia"

Cynthia credits the exercise she has described with helping her render darks and lights and the forms they create. Her previous experience with drawing and painting gave her an understanding of working with values, but this exercise really opened her eyes to what a powerful effect the shapes and spectrum of darks and lights could have in her work. While the color in her cathedral painting is very beautiful, the composition and character of the painting is built upon the shapes of the values.

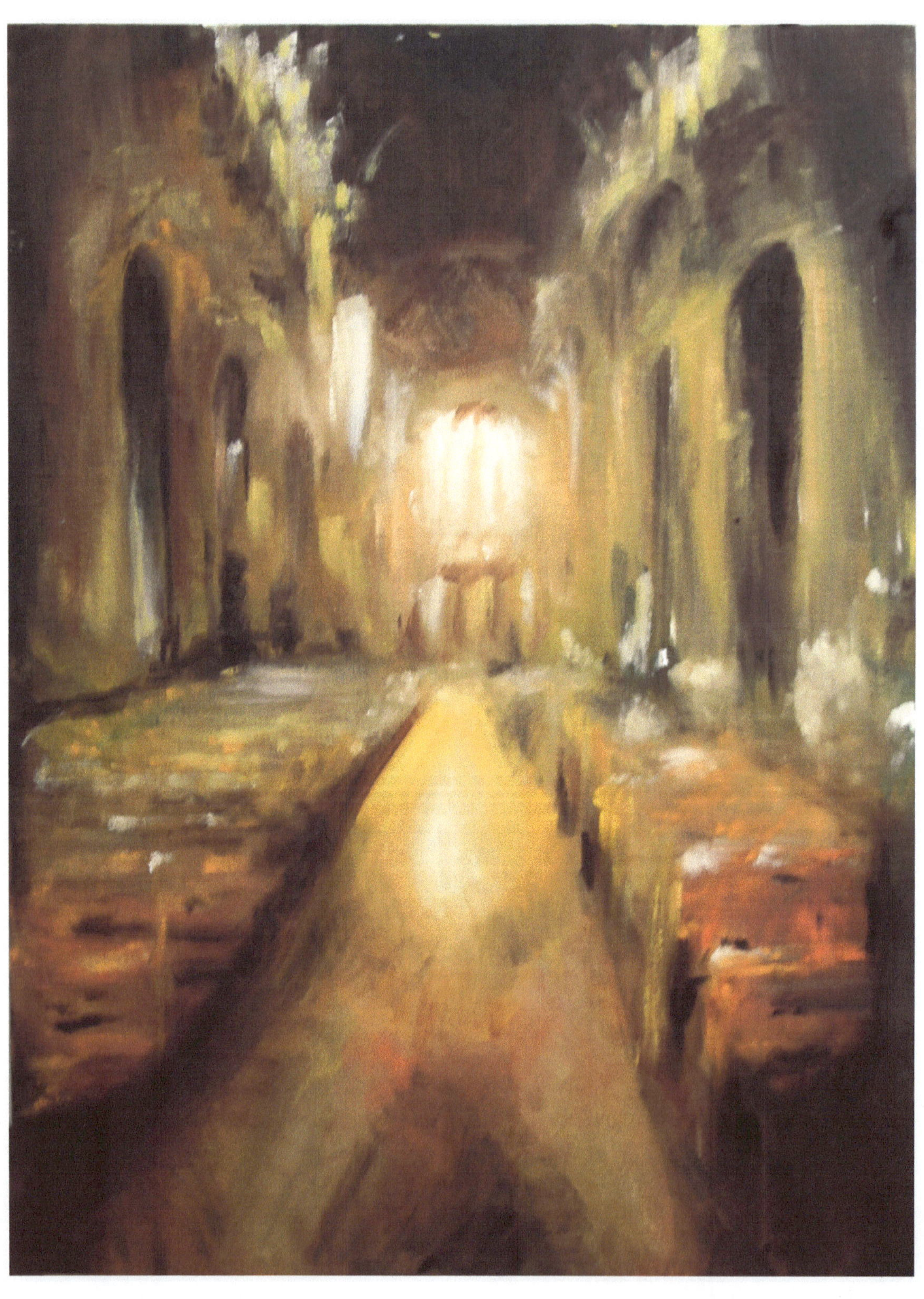

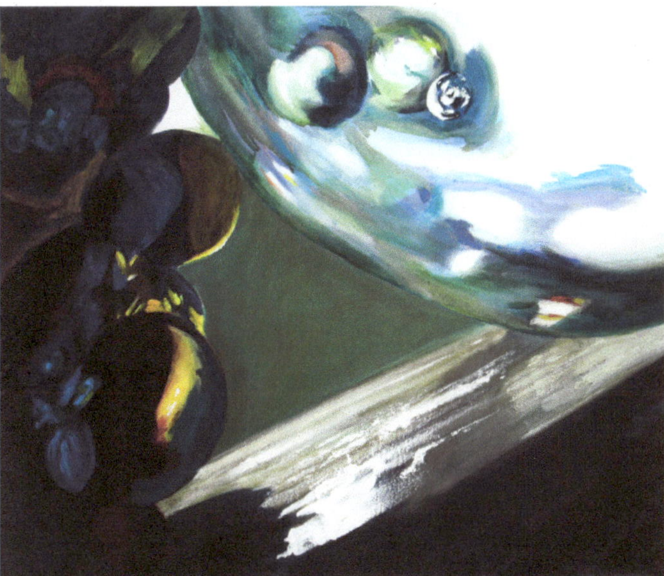

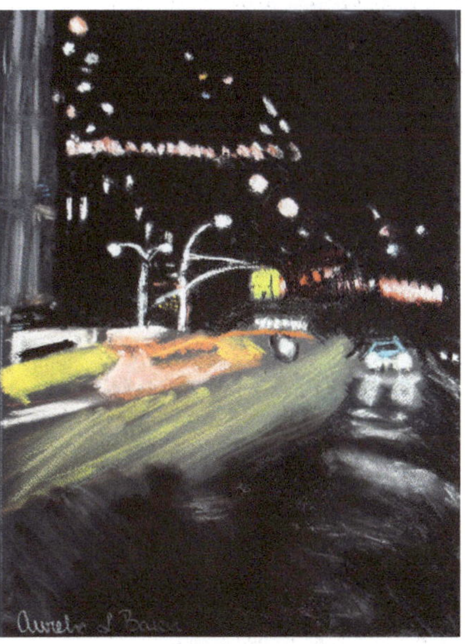

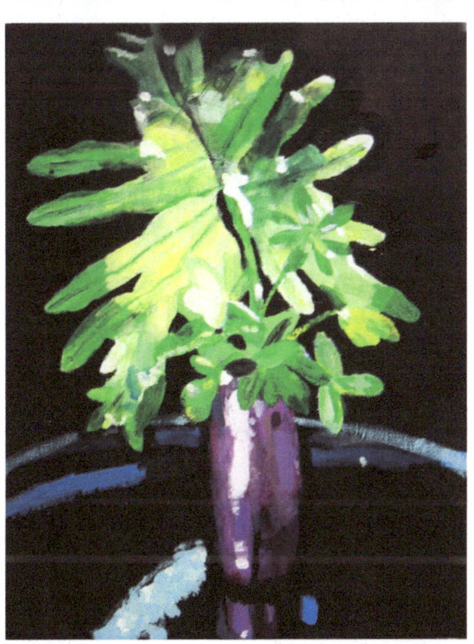

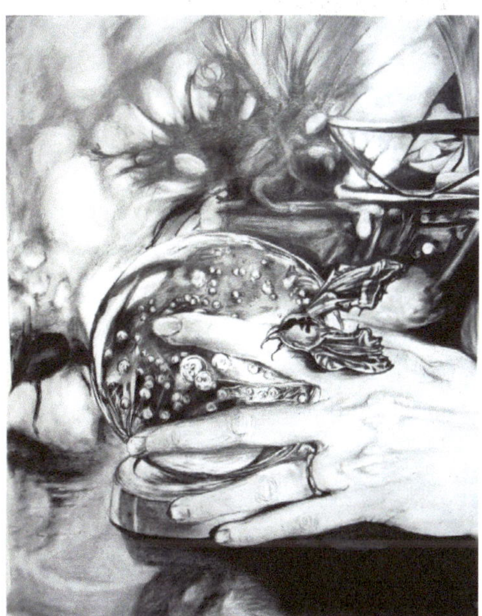

Your Way

Have you ever been in a setting where you can't help but notice the light? Go to a place (inside or outside) that is full of contrasting light and shadows. This could be a room with a window that lets in bright light, an outdoor scene bathed in moonlight, or a setting lit with lamps or neon signs. Squint your eyes to sharpen your focus. Observe the shapes of light and dark. With charcoal or pastel or paint, try to capture what you see.

About Cynthia pg 67

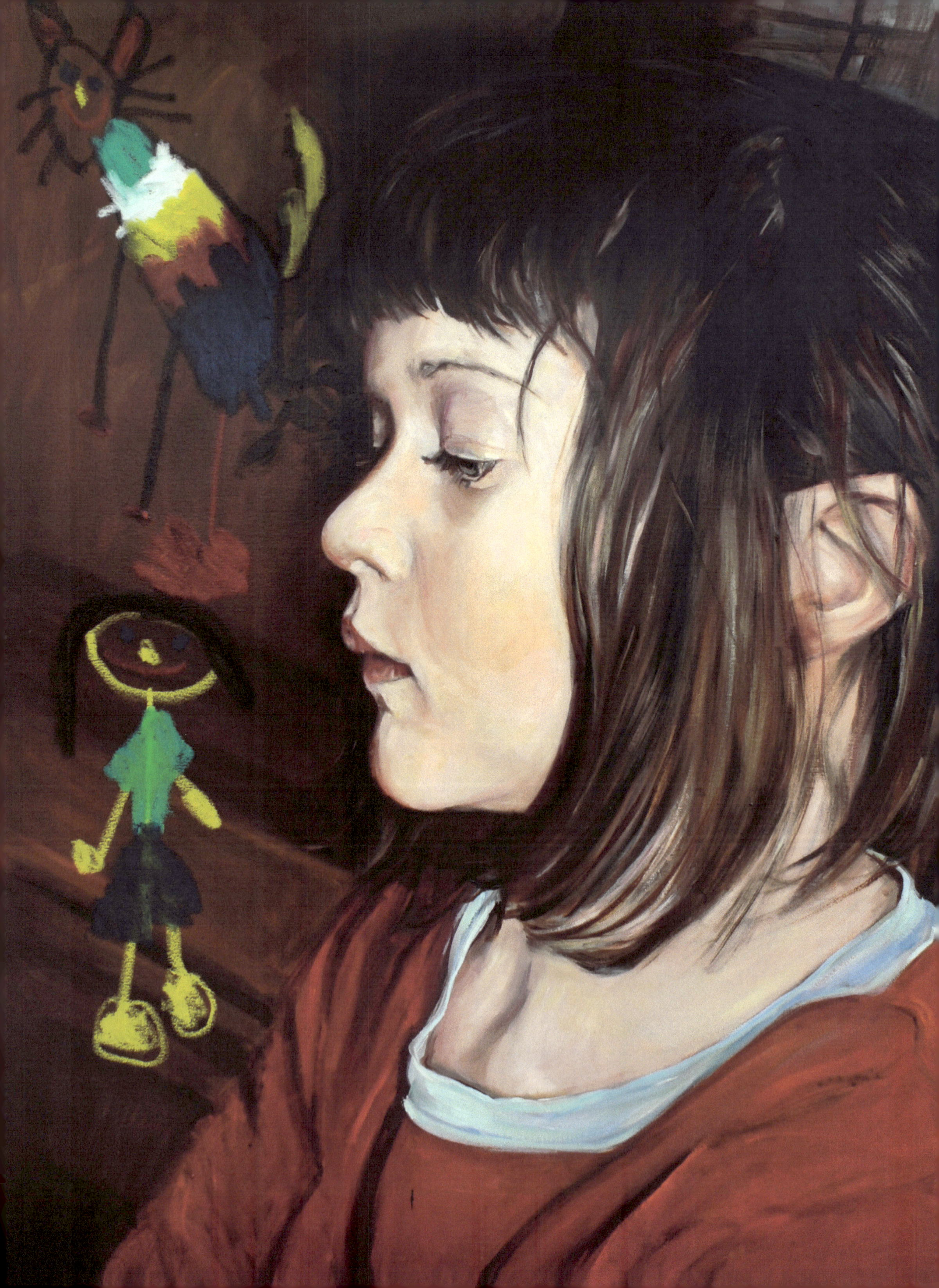

Secret Codes and Symbols

"I love art. I love making something out of whatever I have: pencils, papers, anything. An artist can take anything and transform it.

When you have a big feeling or a secret emotion you can let it out in your artwork. Sometimes when I'm mad I create a piece of art, and it makes me feel better.

-Dianne"

In her piece, Dianne uses painted blocks of color to create depth in her background with line-drawn symbols floating on top. This code of symbols expresses her emotions without giving her secrets away. Only Dianne knows how to interpret them. This can be liberating for an artist, since she is able to express something that is profound and meaningful. We do not need to decode the symbols to enjoy her art. We can let her colors and shapes wash over us and enjoy the entire painting.

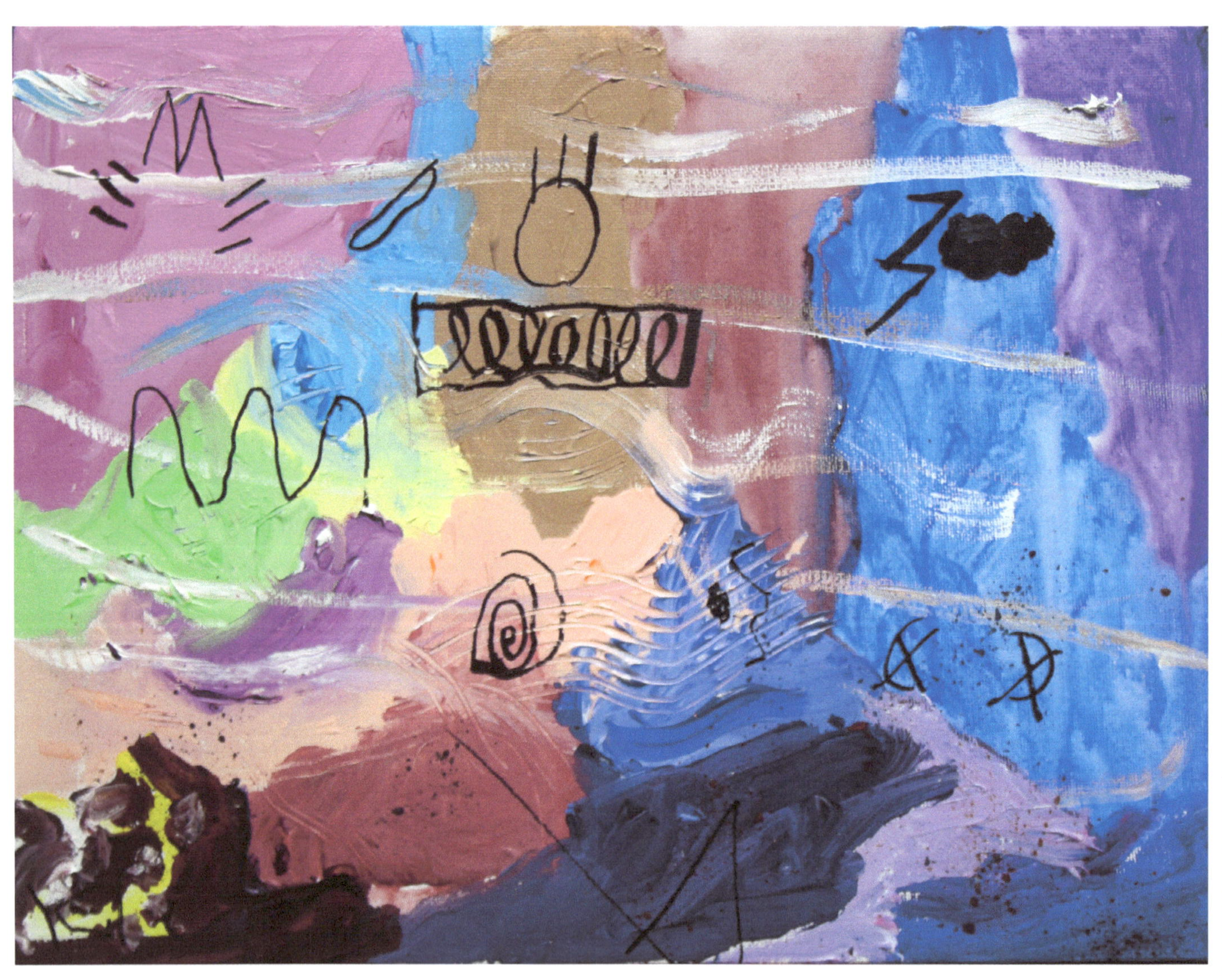

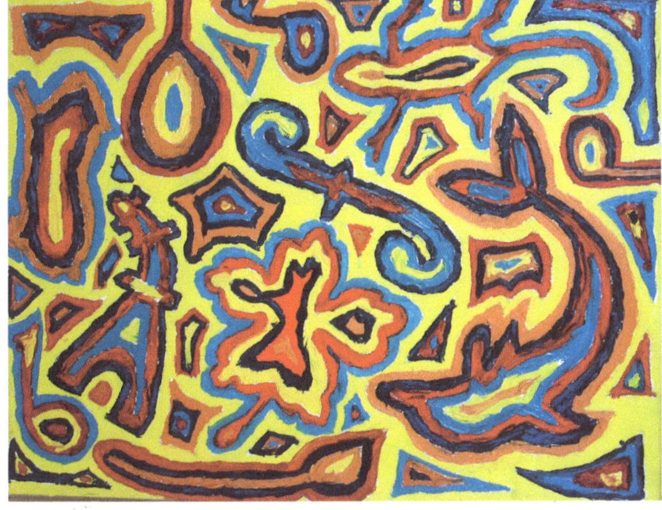

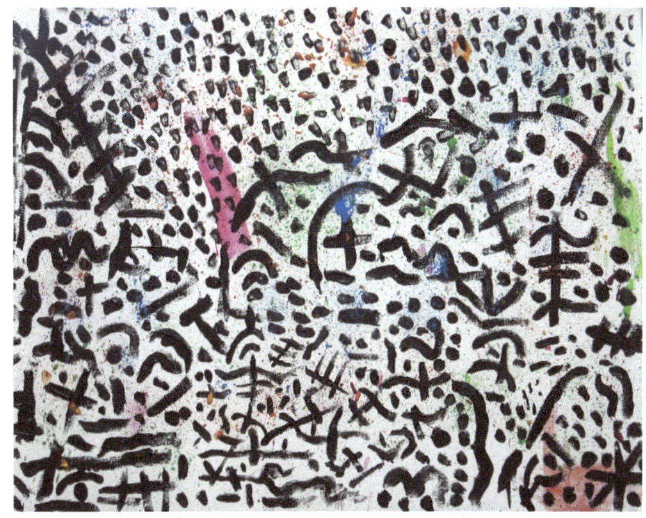

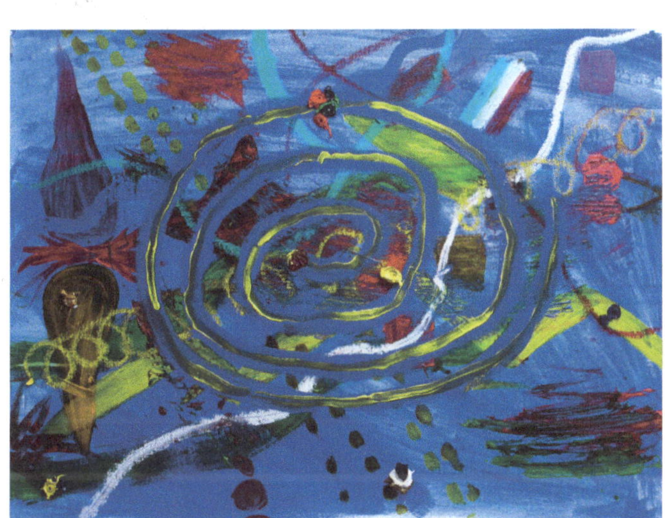

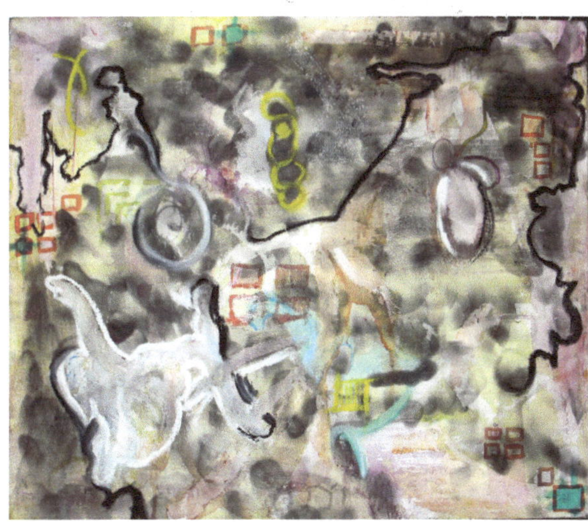

Your Way

Do you have a secret that you want to let out without giving it away? Create your own set of codes and symbols. Assign colors, shapes, scale and texture to each idea you want to depict. Use your symbols to create a piece that contains a private message but can also be shared with others.

About Dianne pg 67

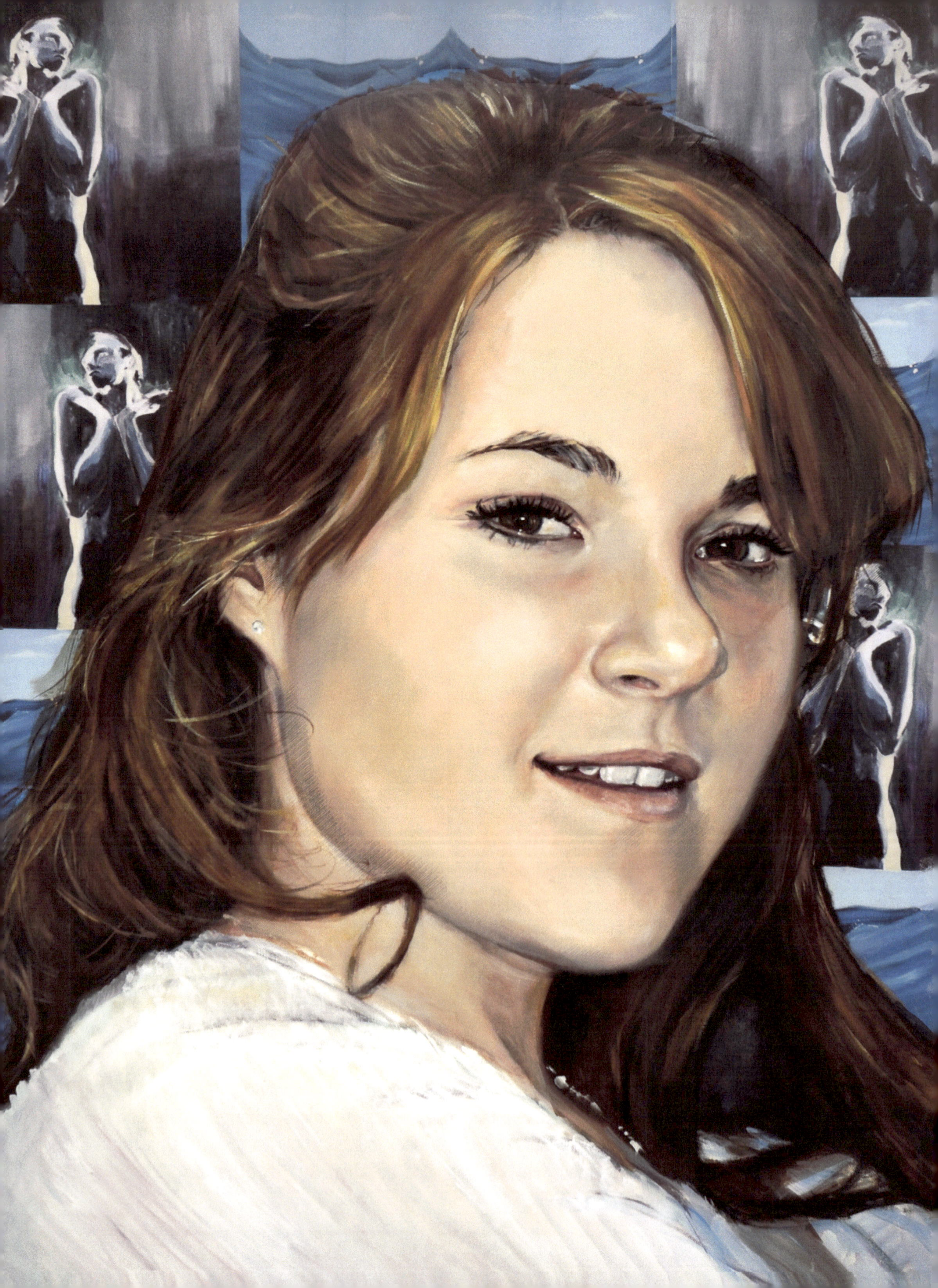

Design

> Color, shapes, line, and texture are everywhere. They create patterns and design elements that communicate on a very basic level, but are very elegant. I sketch and then look around for further inspiration.
>
> As a graphic designer I am communicating with the world. It's thrilling to have others recognize what I am saying with my designs.
>
> -Elizabeth

Elizabeth's book cover design for <u>The Scarlet Letter</u> offers a bridge between the written word and the visual. Her concept is both smart and simple. Bold color and stitches represent the main character in the novel, the seamstress Hester Prynne. The composition and design of the cover provide information about the book, but in a subtle way.

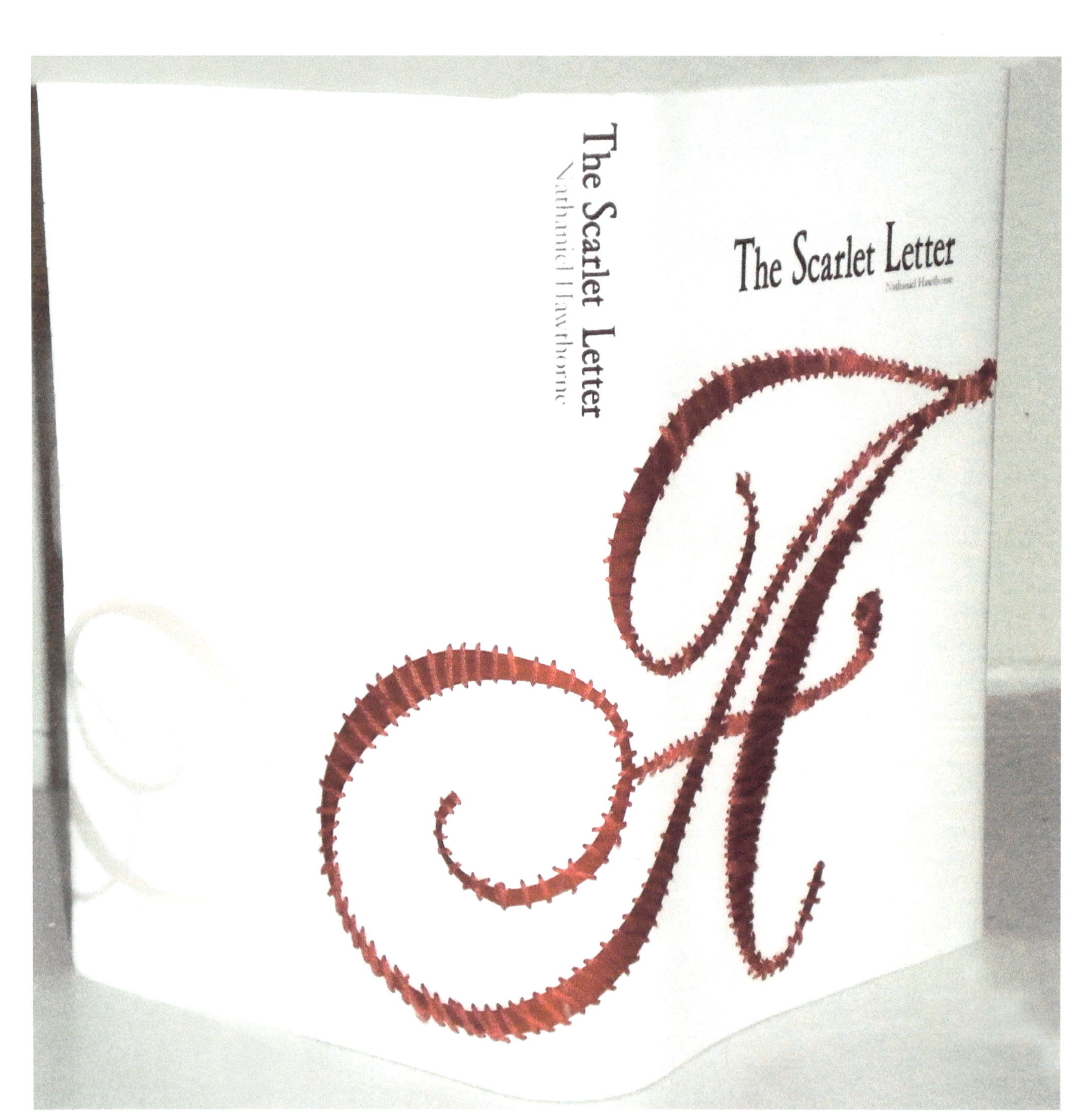

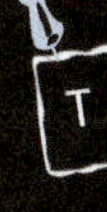

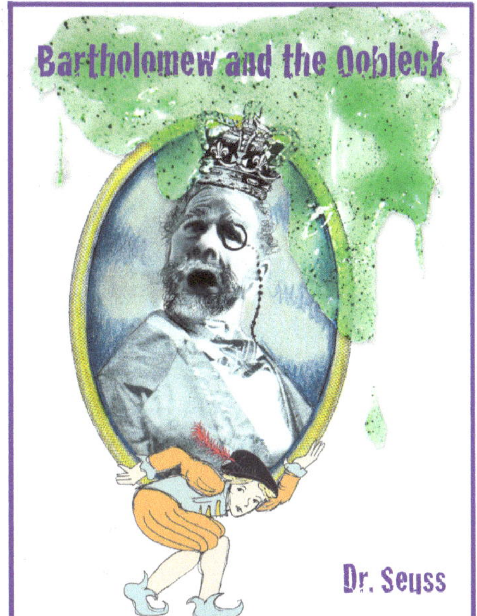

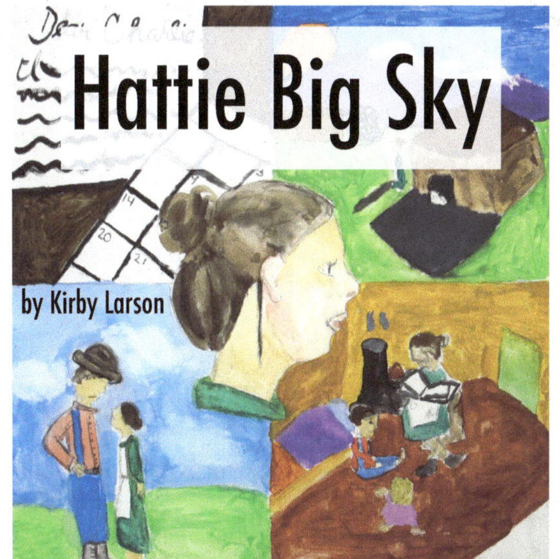

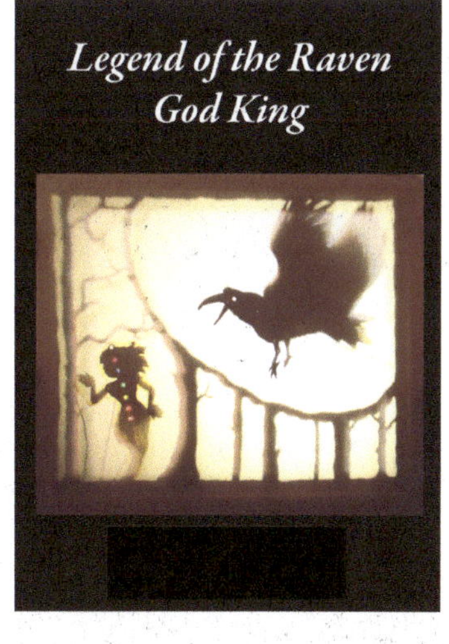

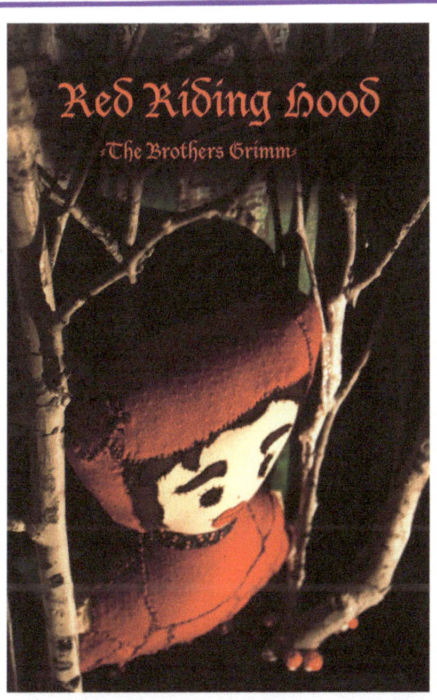

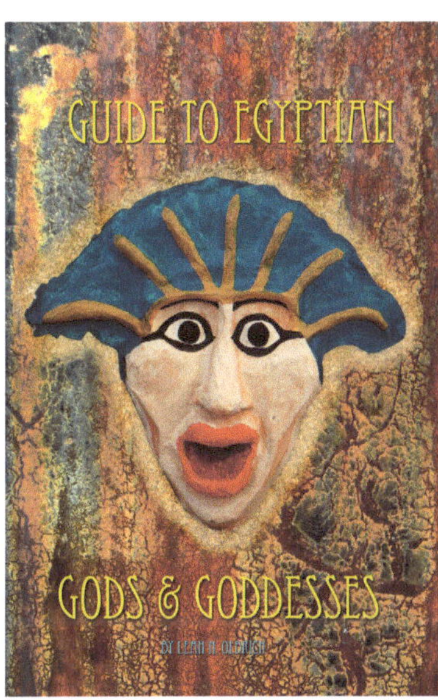

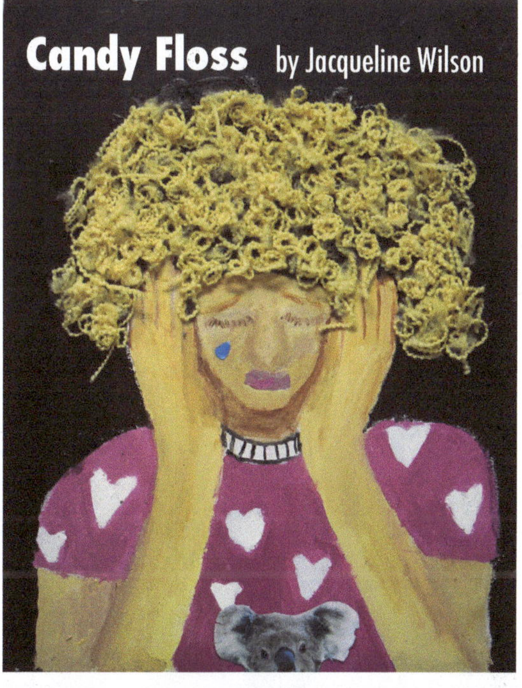

Your Way

Is there a book or movie that left a lasting impression on you? What ideas did it leave you with? Think of an essential theme or scene. How might you visualize it in a simple, straightforward way? Consider all of these things (you might want to write down your thoughts). Select your best idea, then make some sketches. Try to be clear and strong in what you choose to visualize. Make your design "speak" for the book or movie it represents.

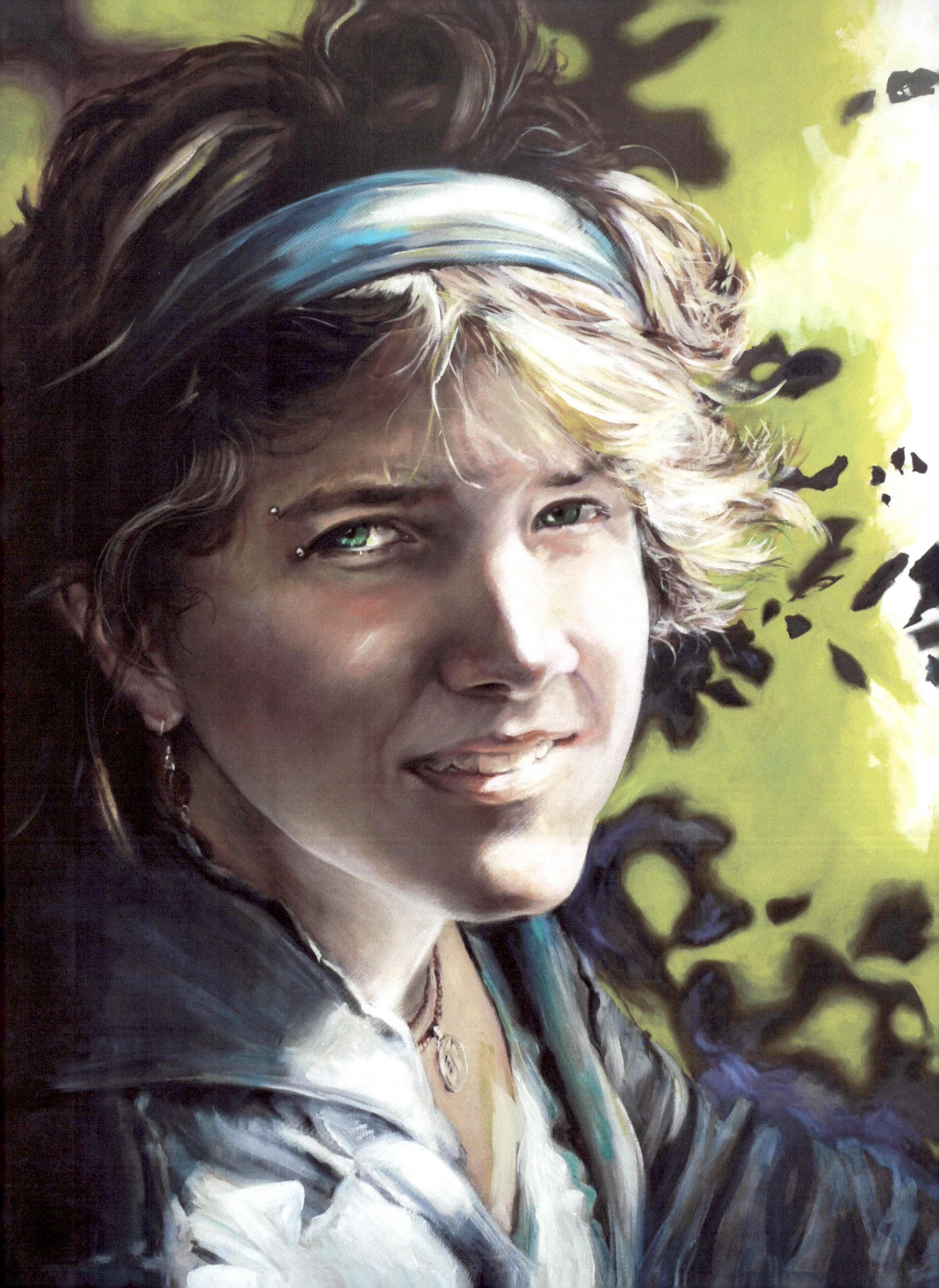

Discovery

"I have always felt connected to the visual world. My thoughts often seem to come in pictures before they come in words. So once I get a handle on the process of seeing, I can pretty much draw anything. However, it does get tricky sometimes. Then I really need to pause and turn things upside down so I don't understand what I'm drawing, so I'm only drawing form. That usually helps.

As I go about my day I may see different things that trigger an idea. Maybe I'll find a leaf on the path, and I really like how the stem curves at the bottom. I find a lot of inspiration in leaves. I often pick them up and discover forms and color patterns in them. They are little characters.

Art does not have to be perfect. I think it's better when it's not. I have found that the pieces I grow to love most are the ones I do not understand at first; the ones that have a slightly grotesque or off-putting element with weird compositions that may be perceived as unsettling. After going back to them several times, I find new beauty within each.

I like magical things. Not rainbows and pink fairy godmothers—their idyllic qualities bother me. The sweet, quiet, magical things that occur in everyday life, like light that halos the fine hairs on smiling cheeks, or a deer in the woods that allows you to get just a little bit closer. They're magic.

-Katherine"

Katherine is very thoughtful and has spent a lot of time exploring her surroundings. We can all benefit from slowing down and seeing instead of allowing our assumptions to guide us. Katherine has embellished simple leaves and urged us to marvel over the complexities of bark. In each case she has altered them slightly to tell us something about them. In her own words, her approach has allowed Katherine to "think of things in a different way and show the importance of the seemingly insignificant."

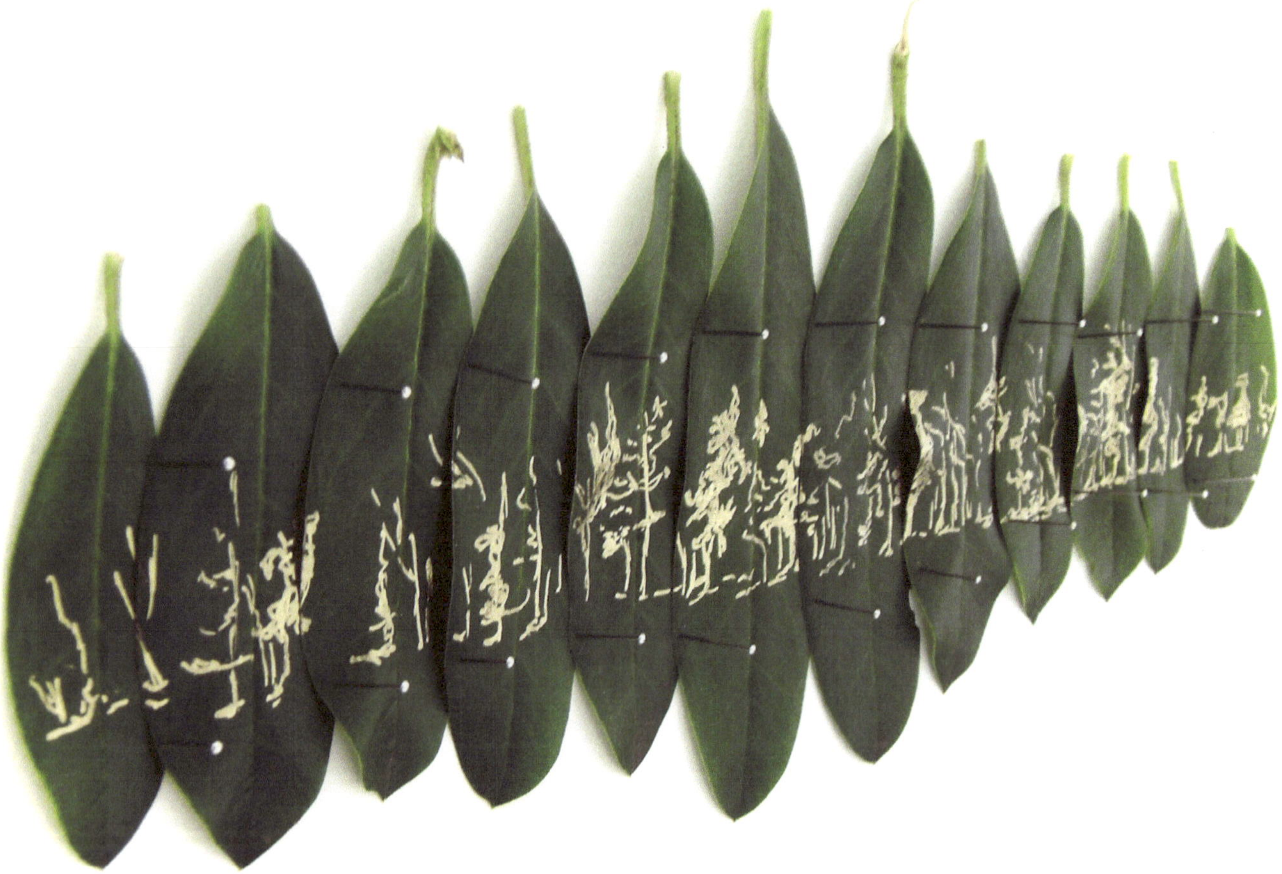

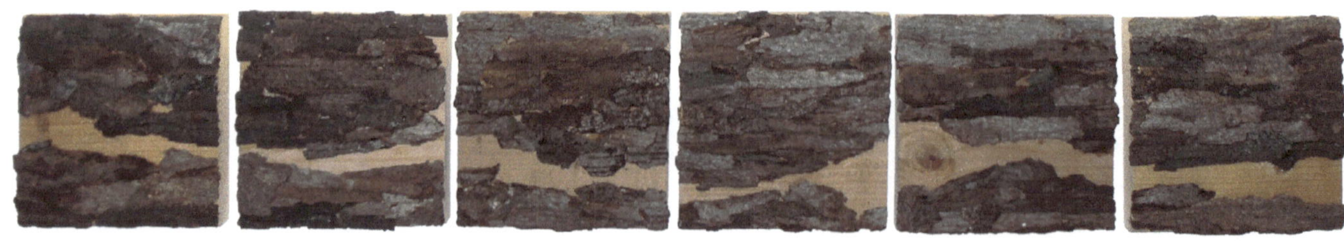

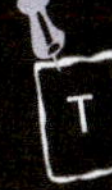

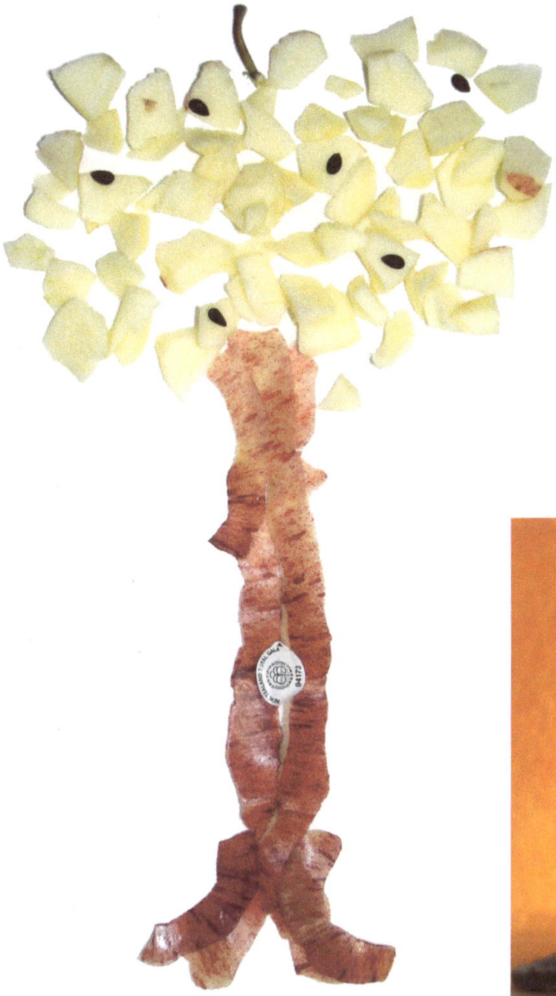

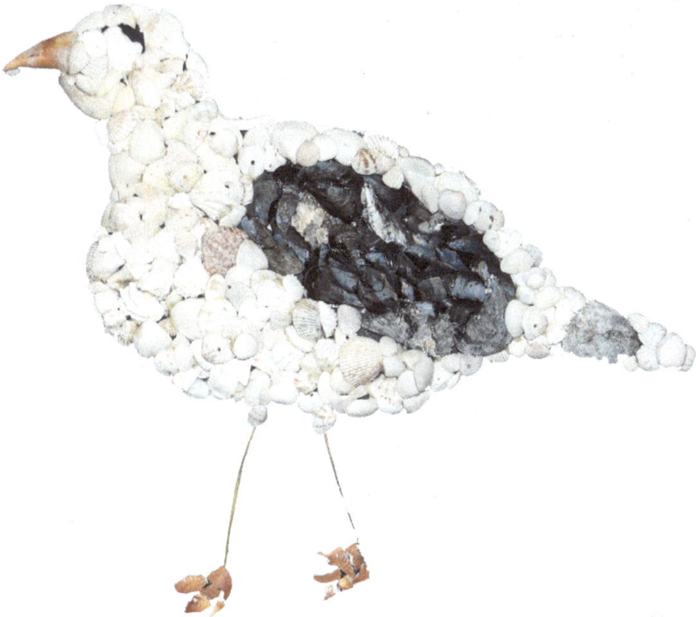

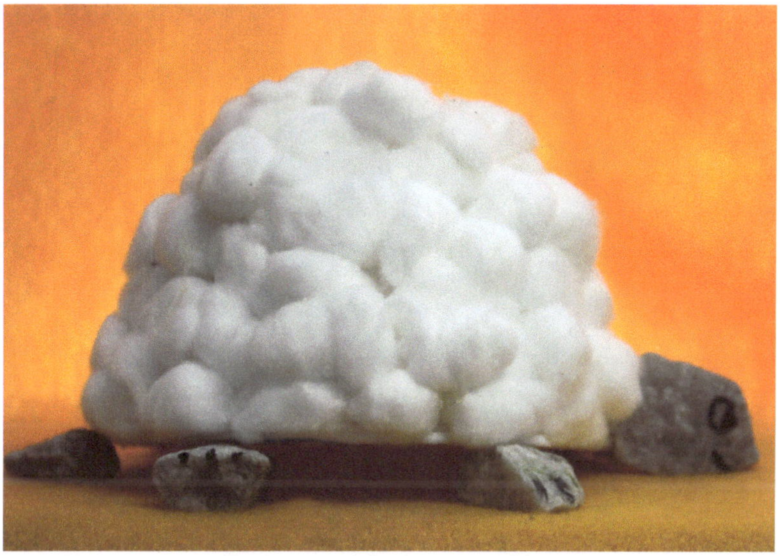

Your Way

Can you look without judgment? Take a nature hike or walk down a city street. Try to become aware of all the little things around you. Make a frame out of paper to help you focus on small details. Make rubbings of different objects to appreciate their textures. Examine nature's discards and bits of trash. Do they share a story? Like Katherine, try to find the "characters." Show off your finds by making them into art.

About Katherine pg 69

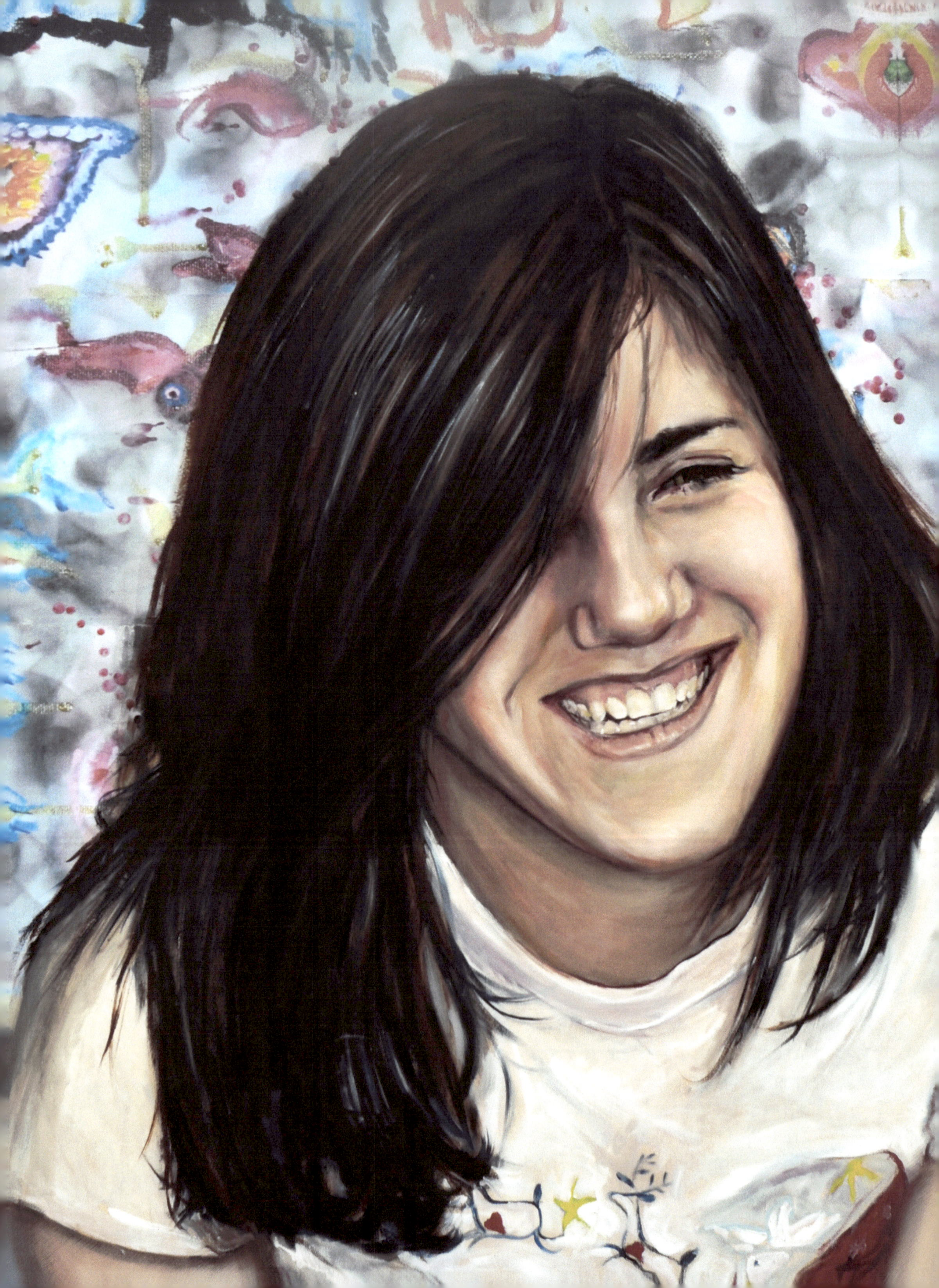

Emotions

"Through art I learned how to express my feelings.

When I started to go to art class, I never thought I could be an artist. My teacher taught me techniques needed to lay the foundation for the emerging artist. I started to grow, and began to feel that maybe I could do this. I could not believe how my art was improving. I started to feel that my paintings had depth and meaning.

Art in middle school was always fun and exciting. Then with the pressures in high school of making new friends, new activities and boyfriends, art began to slip away from me. After going through some difficult times in high school, it was nice to have a place to feel welcome again. Like an old friend, art was there to help ease my spirit. I loved to go to art class, and always left with a smile on my face.

Art has given me the tools to excel through the next phase of my life."

-Ali

Ali's piece invites us to share a moment of anxiety. She has used a variety of materials—layered newspaper, acrylic paint, and oil sticks to create a collage that evokes frenzy. See how she uses the deep black and bright red lines to emphasize the feeling.

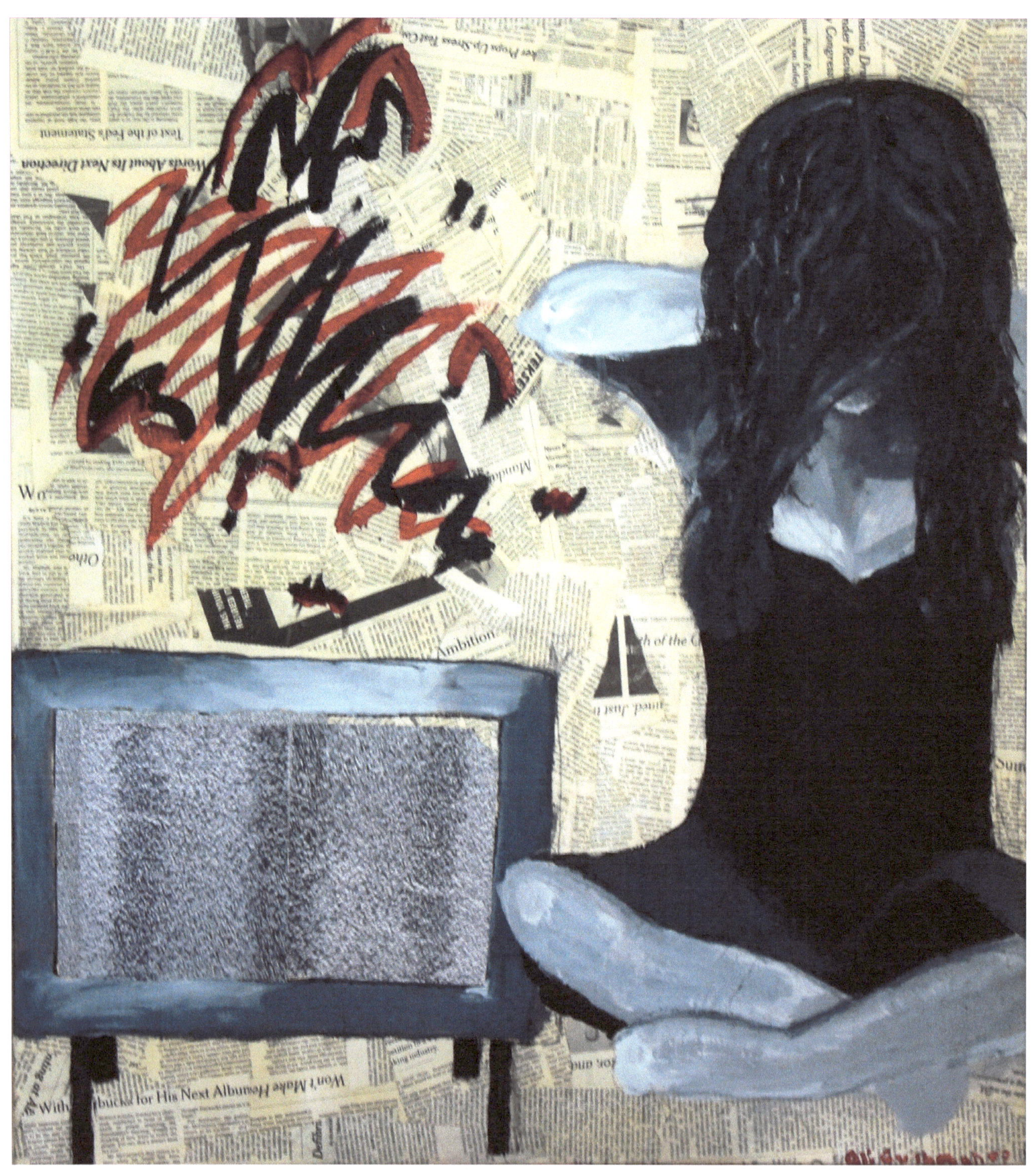

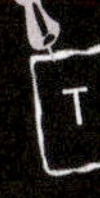

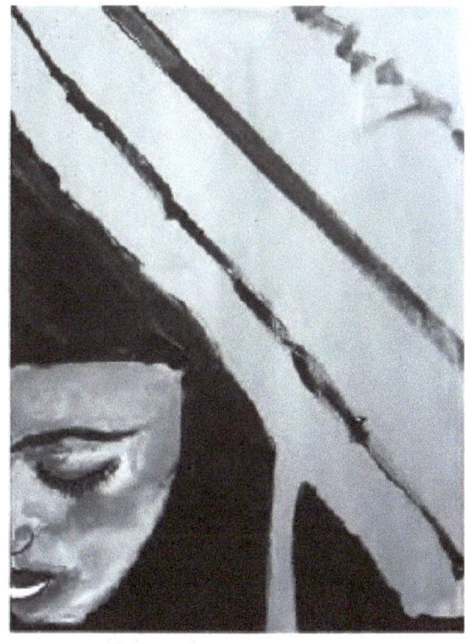

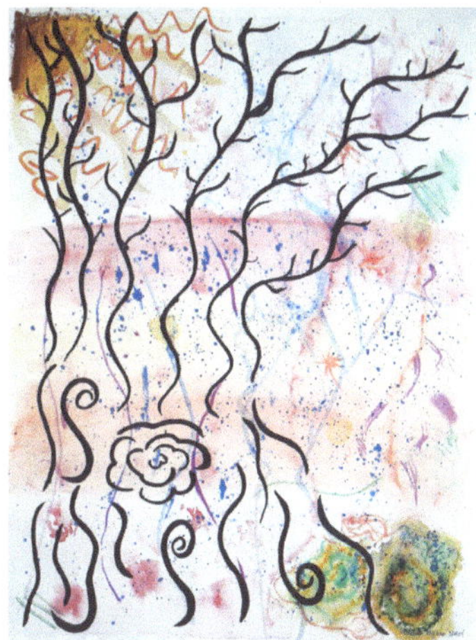

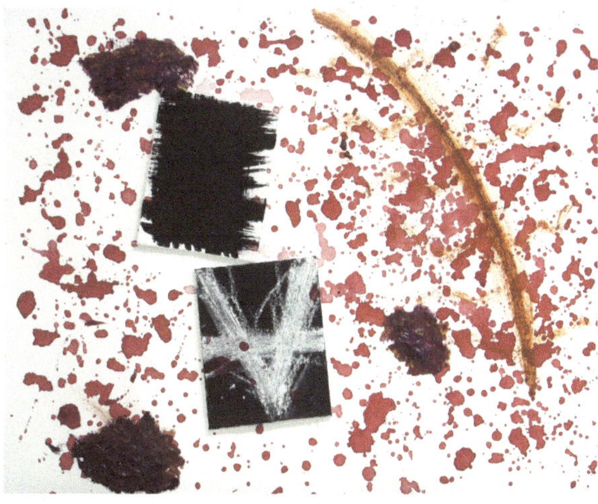

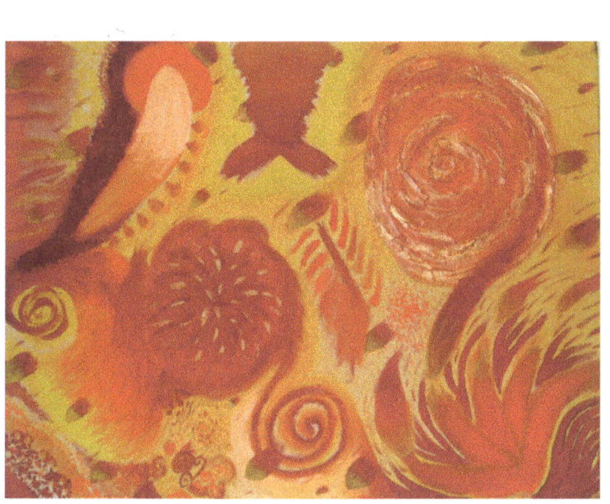

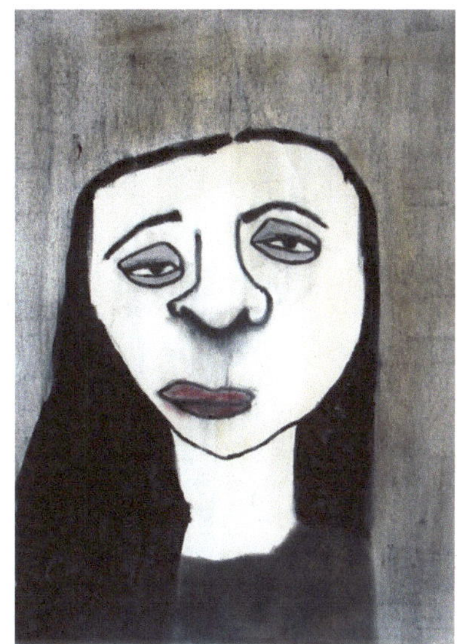

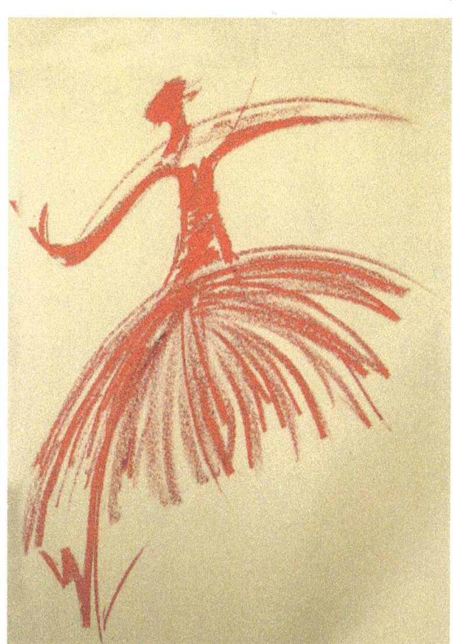

Your Way

Is there an emotion that you would like to express in a visual way? Create a piece of art that reflects your mood. If you find yourself struggling, try this exercise:

Gather several sheets of paper. Write a heading of an emotion on top, like "happy," "sad," or "angry." On each page, using only a pencil, quickly scribble or sketch what this emotion looks like to you. Put aside your judgments. Try not to think too hard about it. Once you complete the exercise, pick the design that you like best and explore what you have created on a larger scale in any medium you choose.

About Ali pg 69

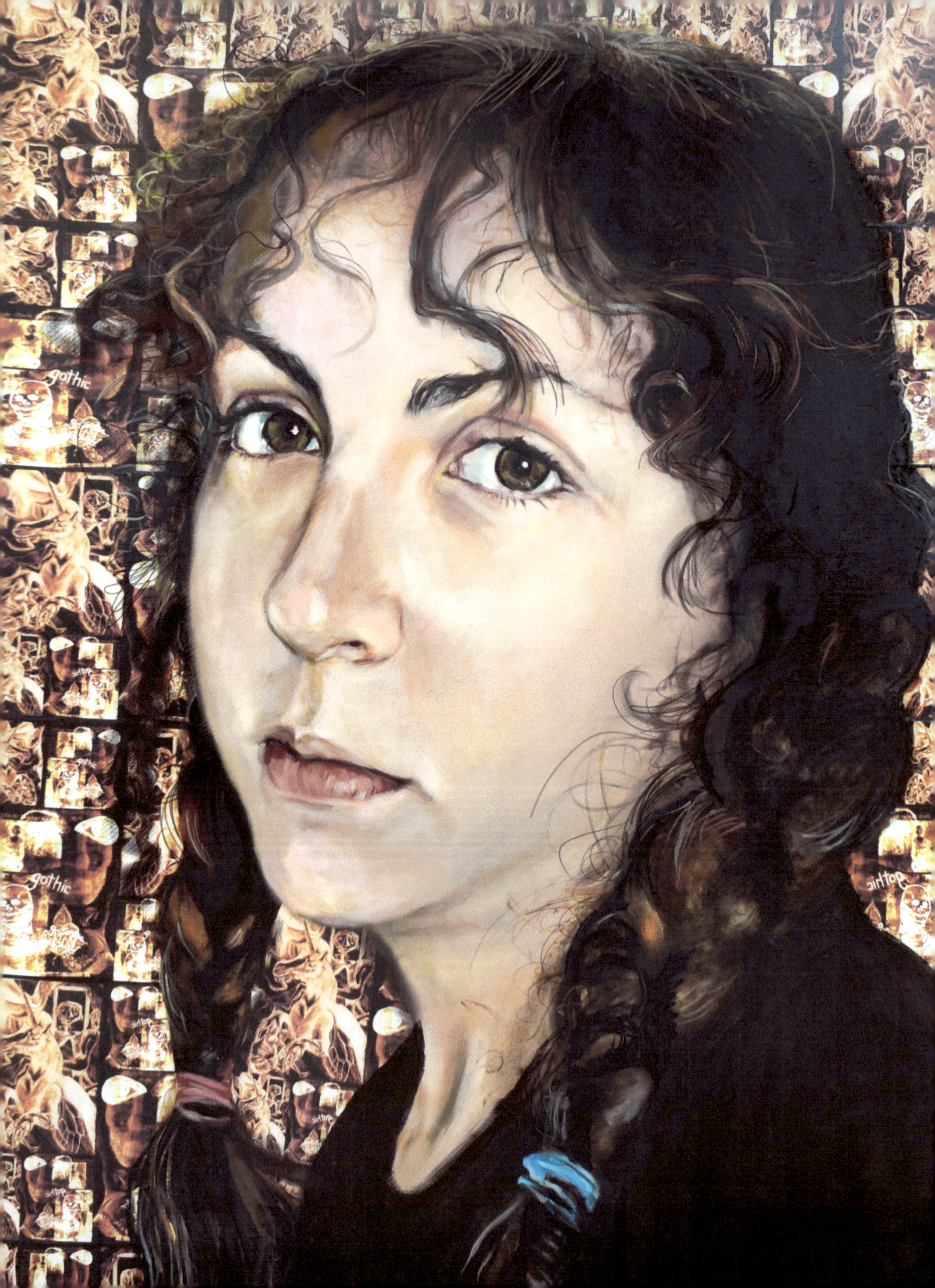
gothic
gothic

Experimenting

"It's taken me a lot of experimentation to get to where I am today—many small realizations.

I used to think it was necessary to justify my art with carefully constructed explanations. Then I realized that this belief stripped my art of the very character I was trying to capture. Now I prefer that my art not be defined at all, because there are endless dimensions to create and explore. There are facets of myself strewn in and among my textural art. I find myself easily and gladly lost in them.

-Leah"

For these pieces, Leah incorporated all sorts of materials into her work, including drawings, photos, yarn and fabric swatches. After scanning them into her computer, she scaled, arranged, and colored them, sometimes adding special effects in Photoshop®. By experimenting with such a diverse set of elements, Leah's work evolves with each new piece.

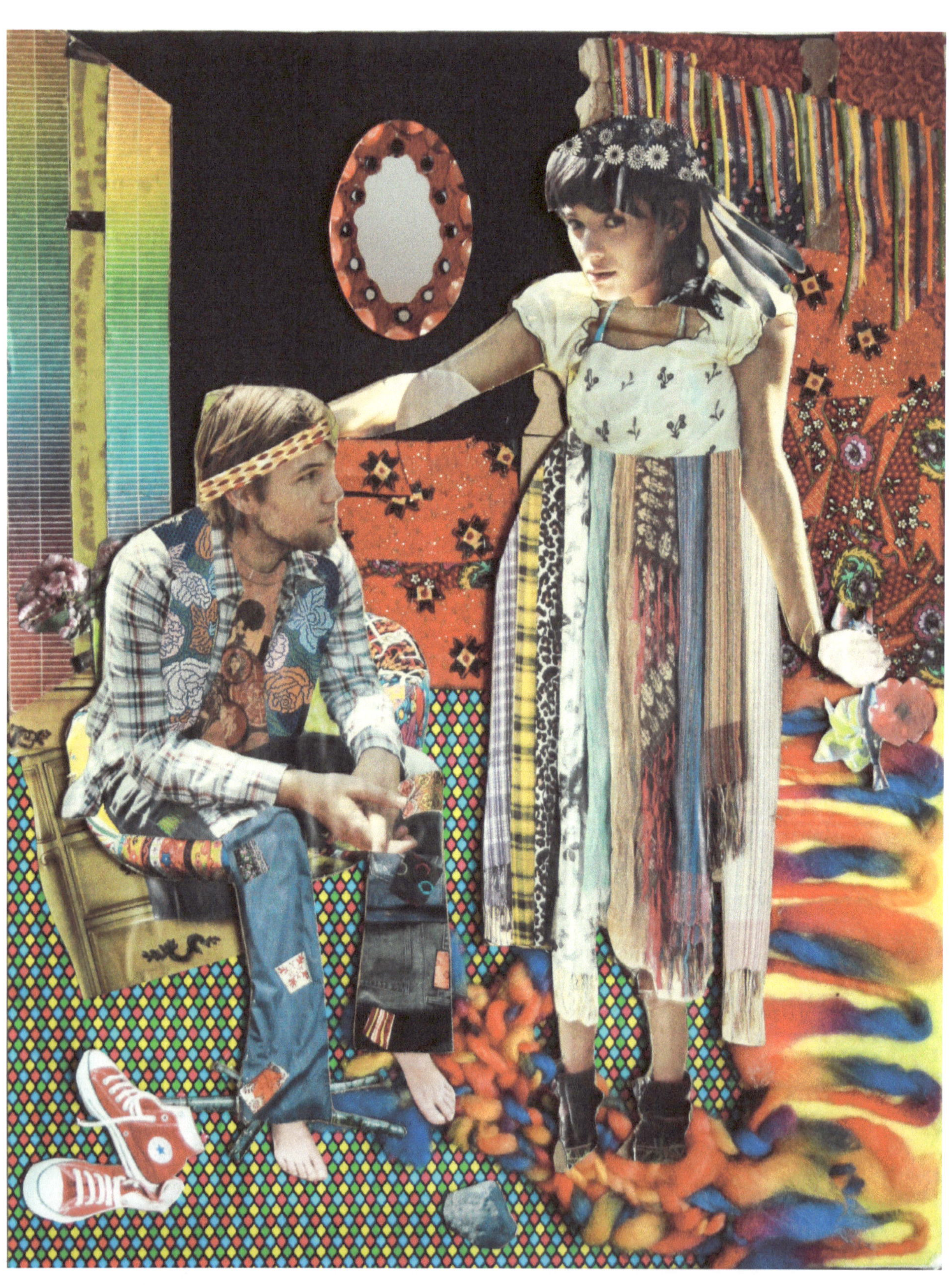

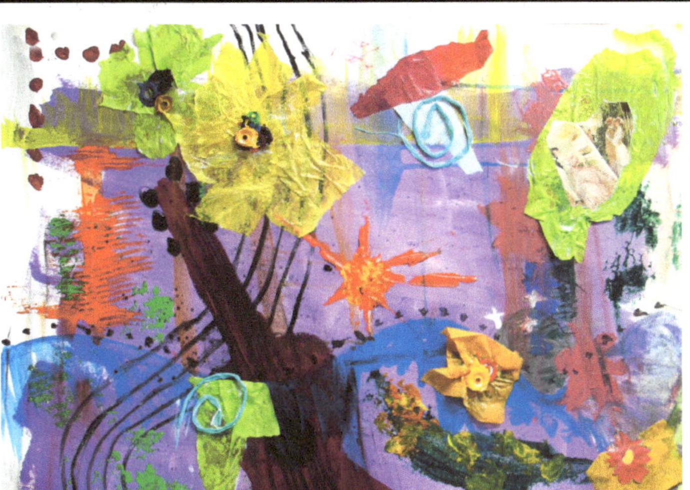

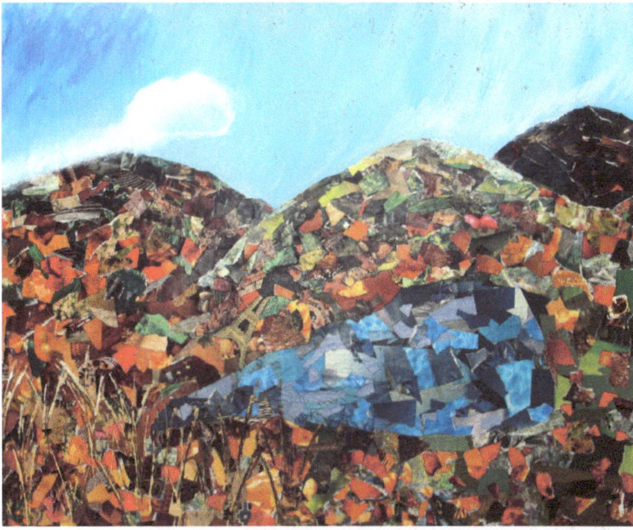

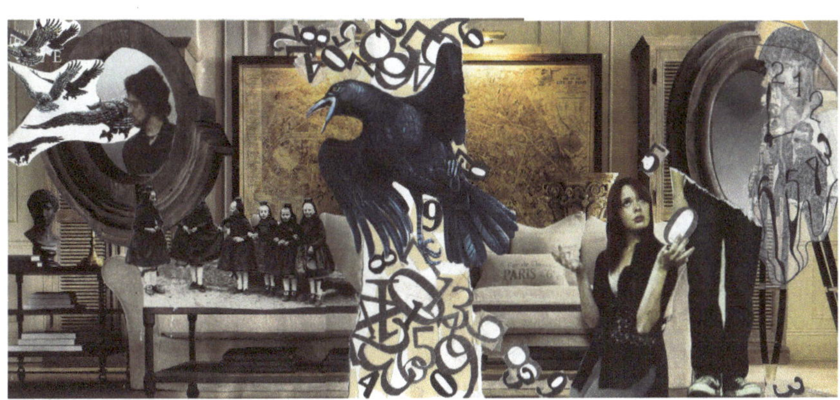

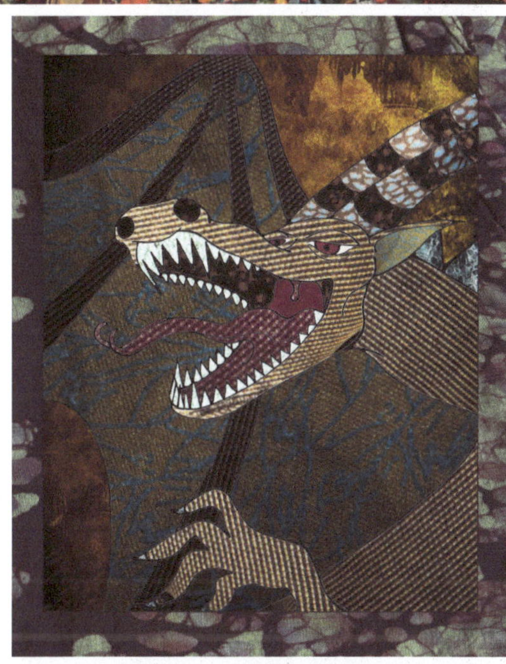

Your Way

Have you tried to put together materials that wouldn't usually mix well together? Like magazine clippings and aluminum foil? Cut out or tear images from fabric, wallpaper samples, magazines, newspapers, labels, and photographs. Look for unexpected materials such as shoelaces, cereal boxes, or anything else that attracts you. Draw and paint additional images. Collage them together in a way that pleases you. You can use a scanner and a computer application like Photoshop®, or not.
Experiment!

About Leah pg 70

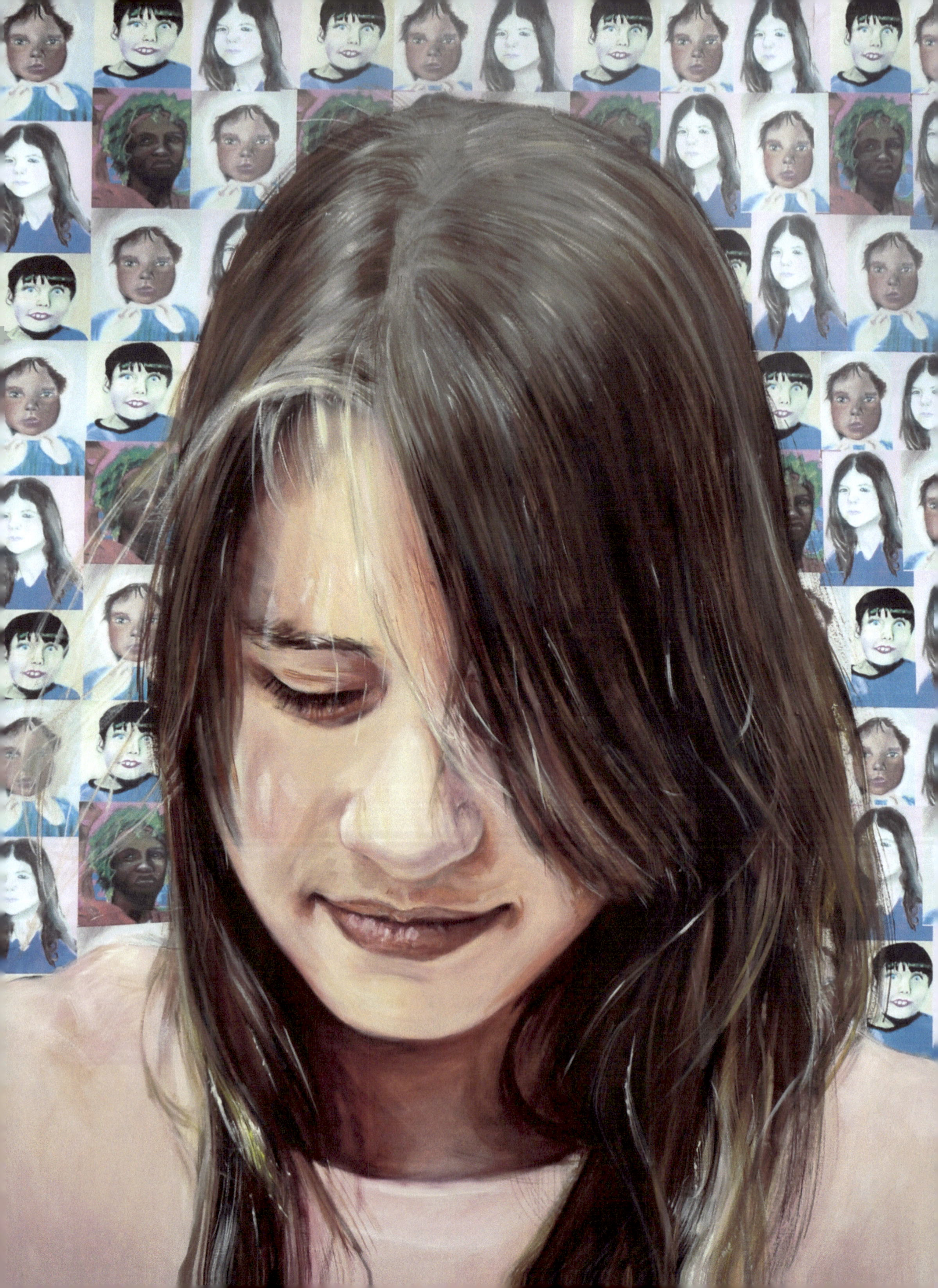

The True You

Art helps me lay out what's in my head.

When I was little, art felt like glue and macaroni. Now I let my hands and eyes blend in harmony. You can draw what you feel and no one will ridicule you or tell you it's silly. Art helps me see things clearer and it makes me feel free. Your art gives people a better insight into what you're like, and it helps them to see the true you.

Sometimes art speaks louder than words.

-Rachel

More than a traditional self-portrait, Rachel's piece enables us to get a feel for all the diverse elements of her identity. In a very real sense, she gives us a tour of what's inside her head.

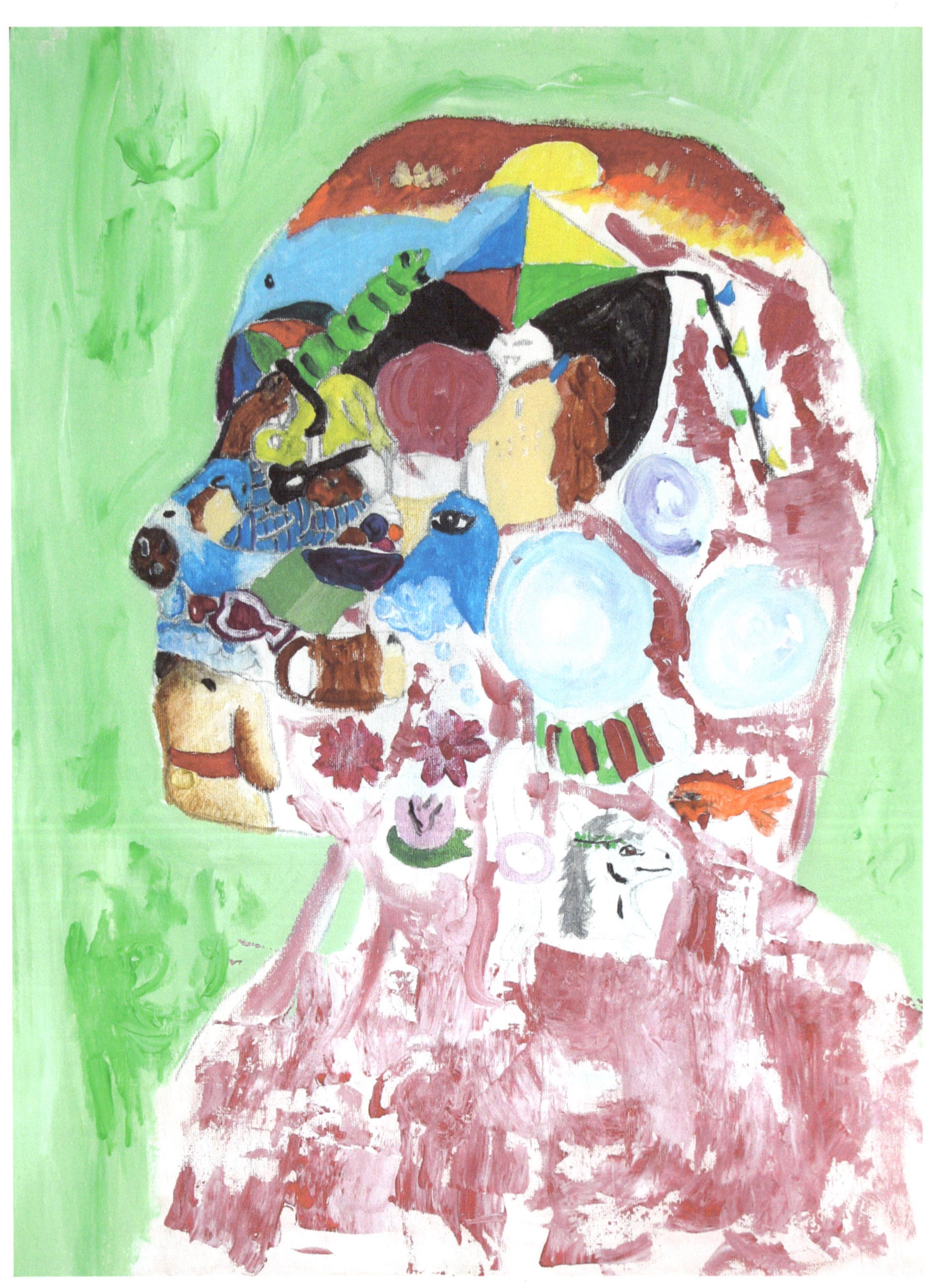

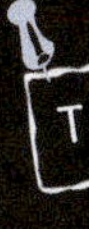

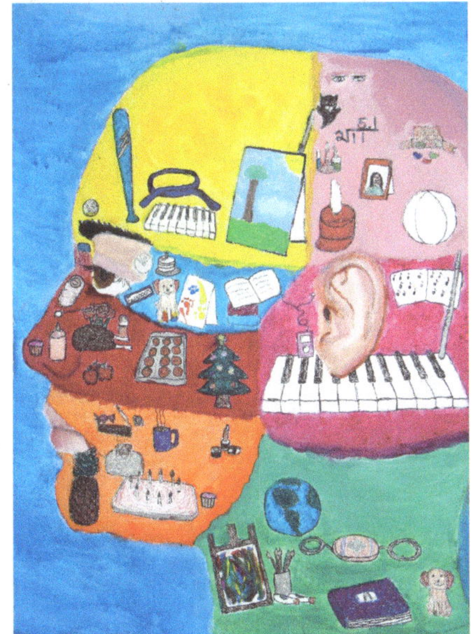

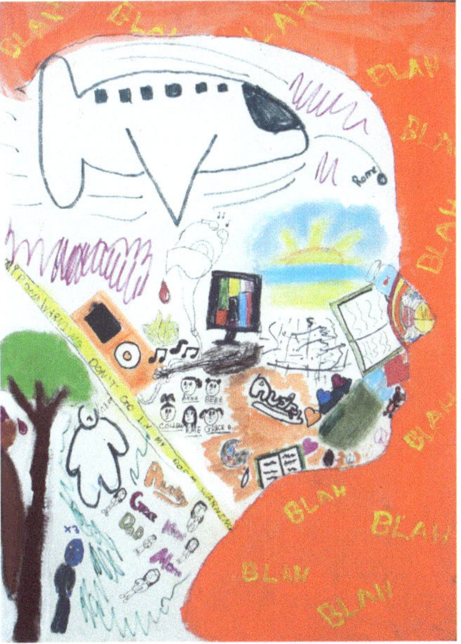

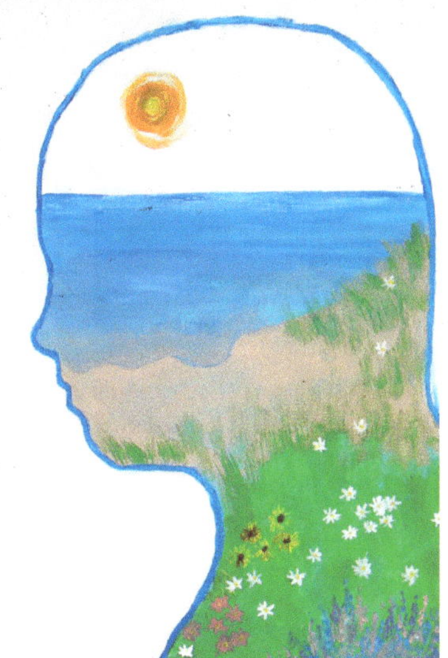

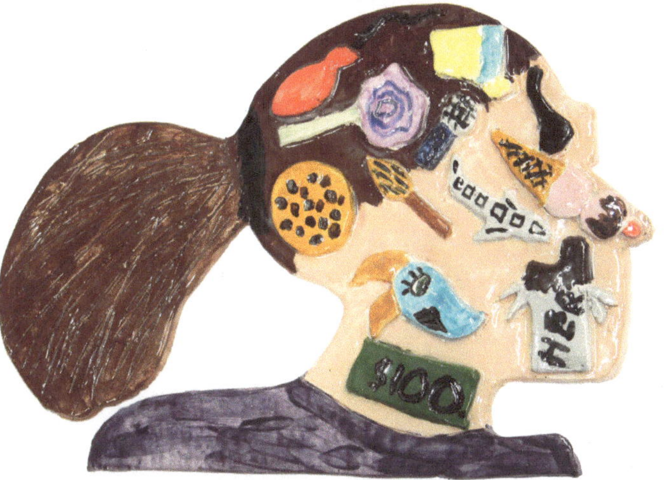

Your Way

What's on YOUR mind? To make a piece like Rachel's, hang a large piece of paper on a wall. Use a lamp to shine a light on the paper from a few feet away. Sit sideways between the paper and the lamp so you're not facing either one. Your profile will cast a shadow on the paper. Ask a friend to trace it. Now you can make a list of your favorite things, your deep thoughts, or both. Fill your profile outline with the images that come to you. Your self-portrait can be a painting, a drawing, a collage, or even a sculpture, like Martha's.

Allow the true you to shine through.

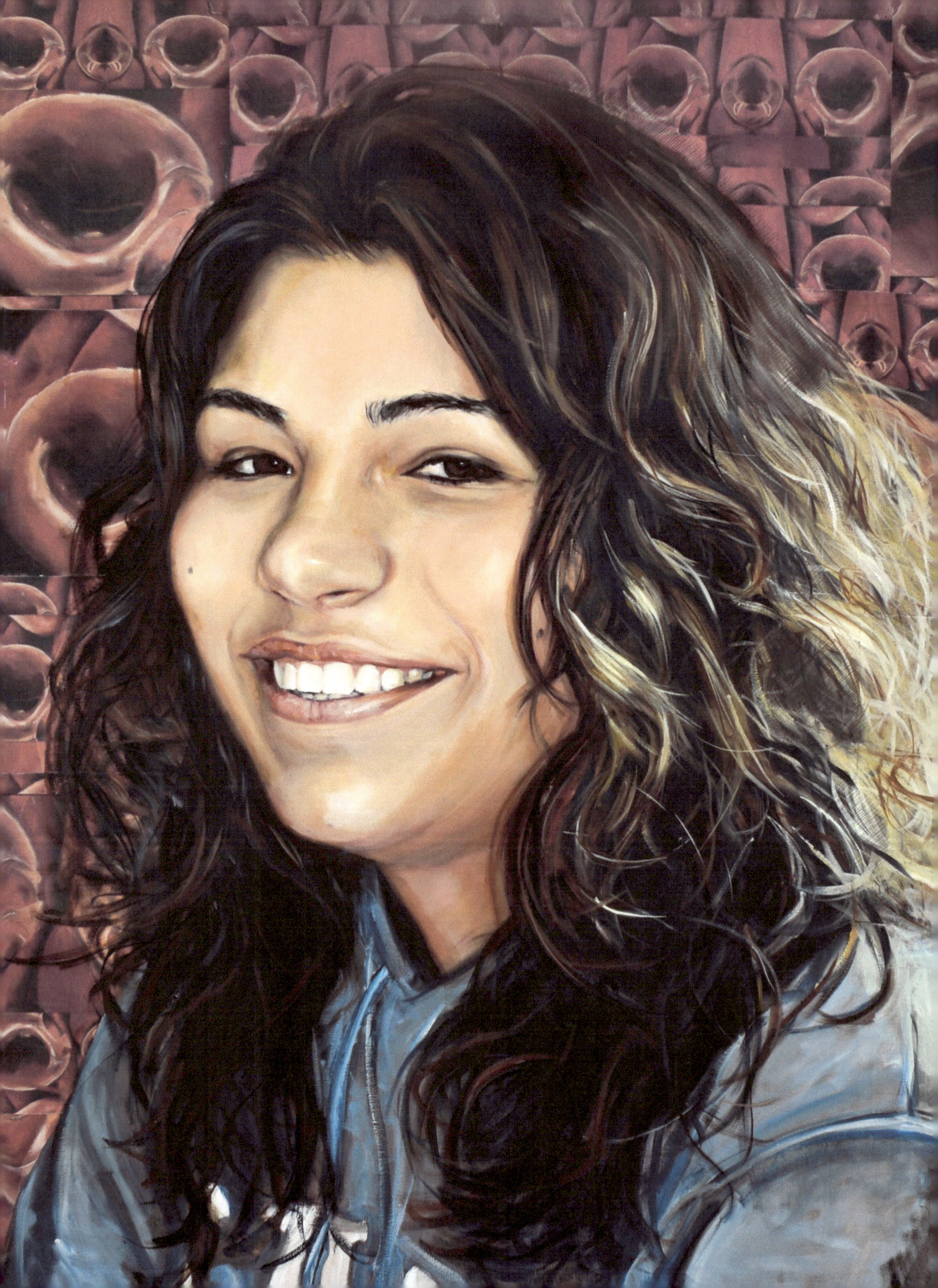

Blending Interests

"For me, art is so much fun because you can combine it with other interests.

With pastels there are so many shades of each color, which makes them so much fun to blend. All the colors easily work together and form anything you can imagine.

I'm interested in science, art, and making special art for my friends and my family. I've painted garden scenes and red blood cells. For my sister, I painted a still life of her mementos. I painted a portrait of my grandfather for his birthday. I spent many weeks painting this portrait. I did my best to portray all of his facial characteristics accurately. I remember the day I gave Poppop the portrait. I couldn't wait to give it to him! I know he truly appreciated my gift.

-Tara"

Tara recognizes what is meaningful to her, and combines those things to inspire her artwork. She shows us that human lungs are not so different in appearance and function from a coral reef. Also, that favorite things and favorite people inspire meaningful work. Tara is quite passionate about her favorite medium, pastels.

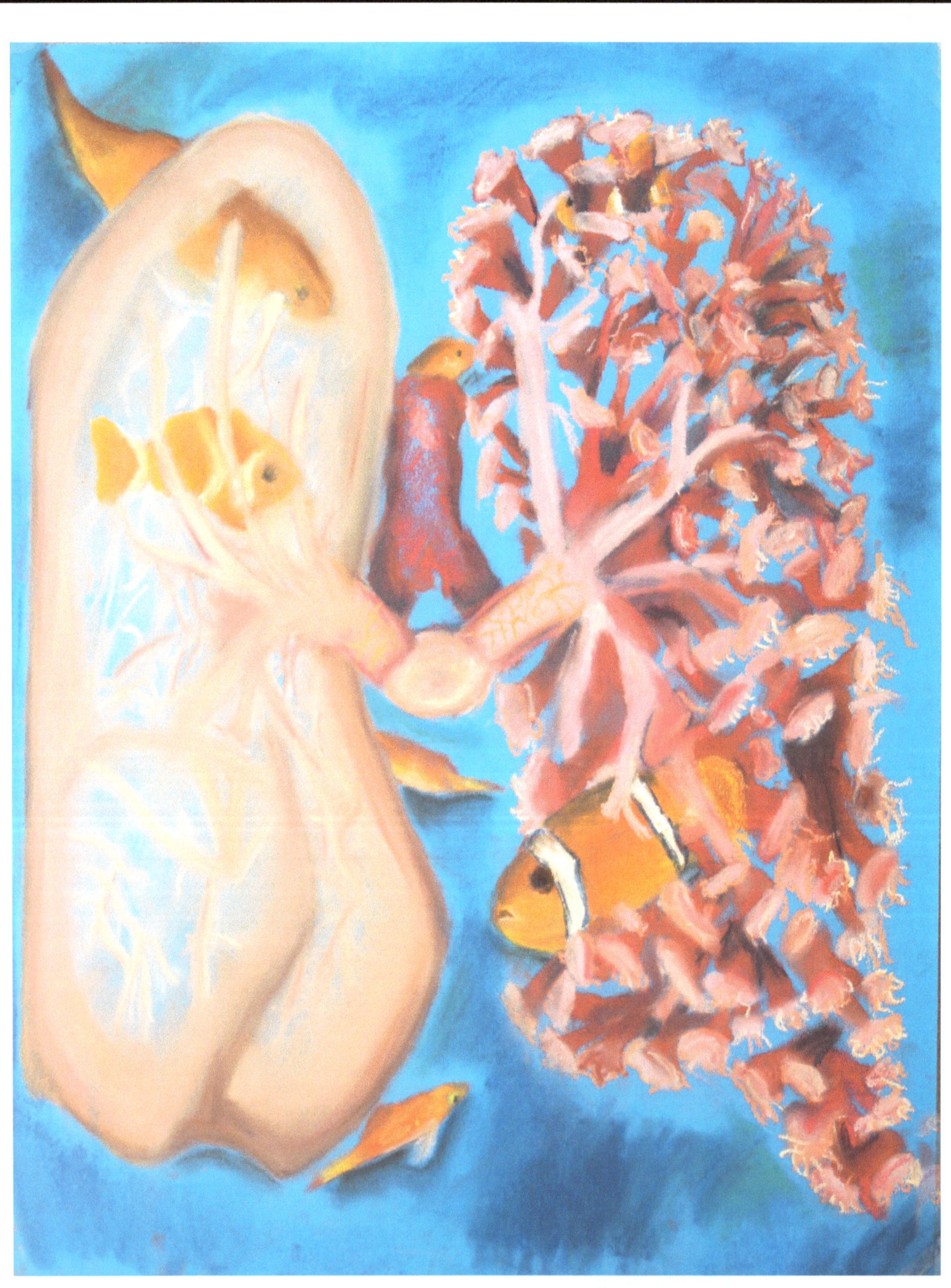

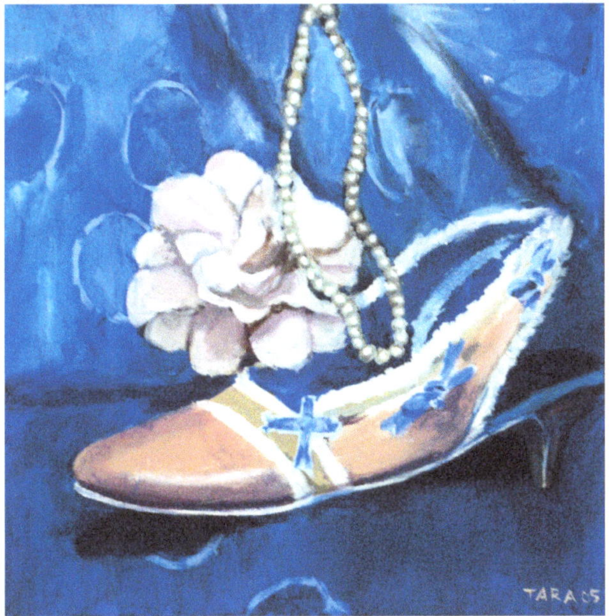

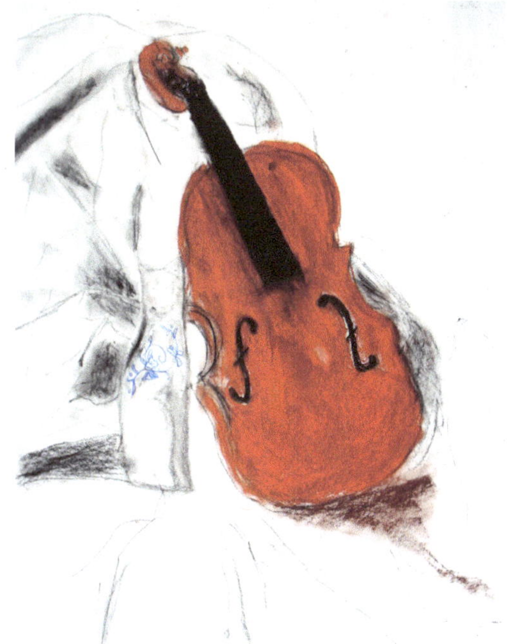

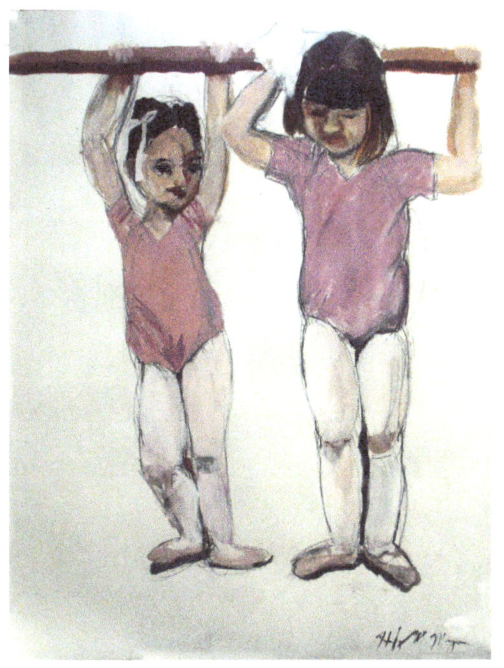

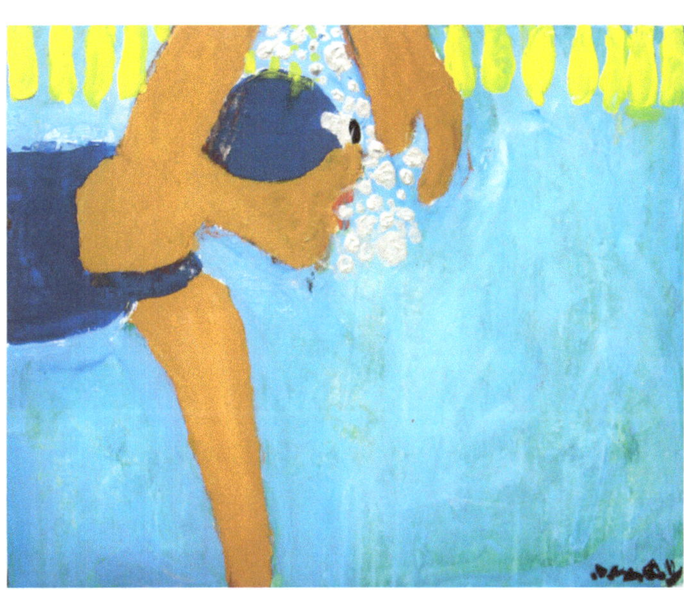

Your Way

What are the things that excite you? What or who do you appreciate most? What is your favorite creature, subject in school, sport or hobby? What is your favorite medium? Consider your passions—your favorite hobbies and interests. Is it possible to combine them in an visual way?

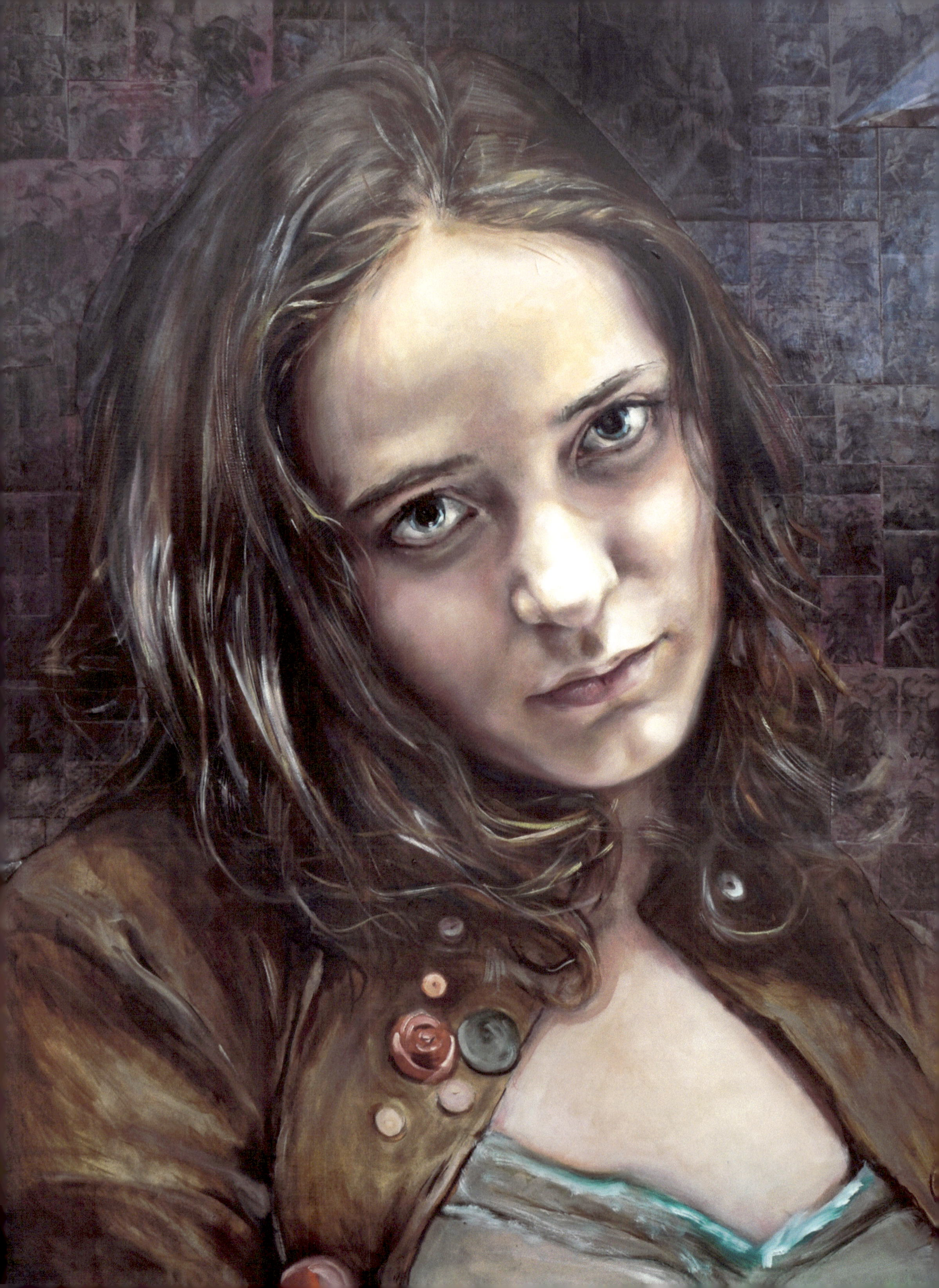

Sketchbooks

"Art is like home to me, and my sketchbook is the place I bring everything that is important to me. When something upsets me, I explore my feelings in my sketchbook. When a quote or a song lyric inspires me, I bring it to life in my sketchbook. It holds what I think, feel, and want to remember.

I use my sketchbook to plan larger works, as well as integrating my writing with my visual art. It's the place I go to work things out.

-Taylor"

Taylor's sketchbooks are filled with all sorts of secret folds and panels. Her pages are collaged, painted, cut out, laced, and textured. She has even used boxes as covers and has sewn her pages right into the boxes. Taylor's books house spectacular tiny finished works and fragments of potential projects. Every page is unexpected and different from any other. Every page hints at the possibility of a new piece that can grow from its rich content.

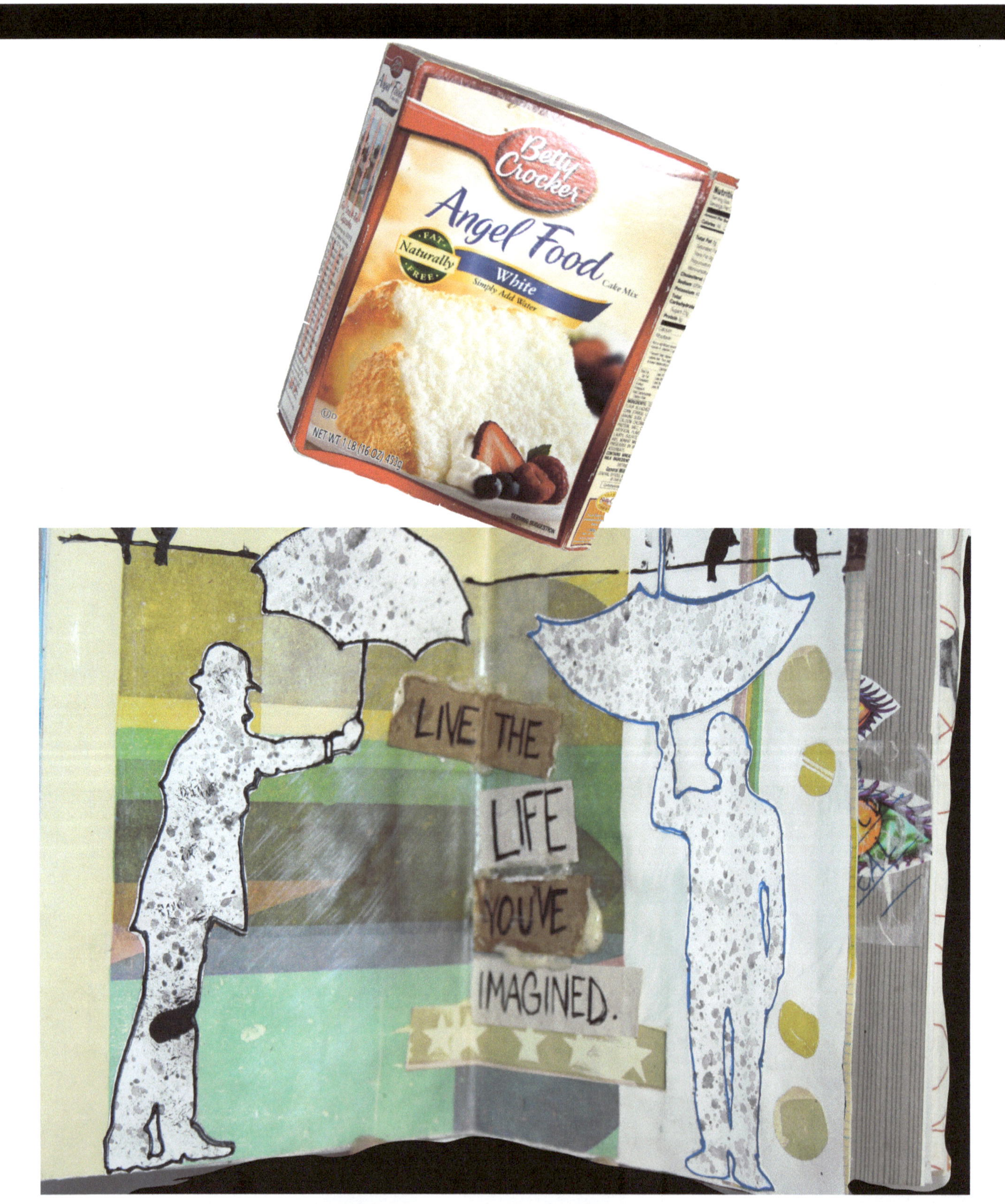

Inspired By Taylor

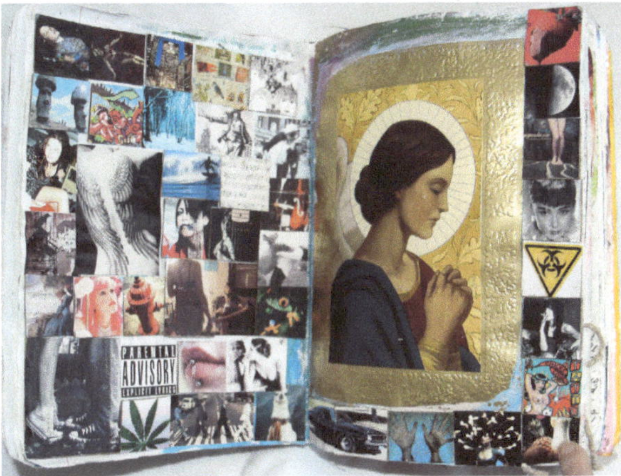

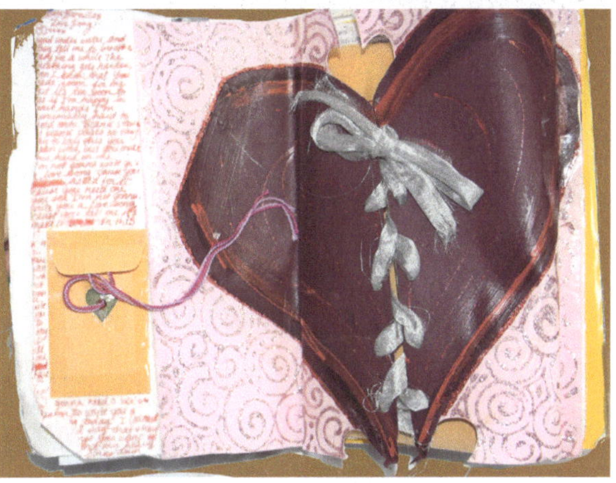

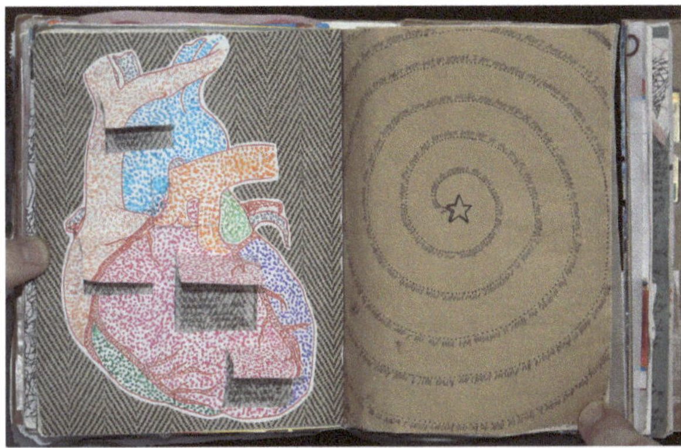

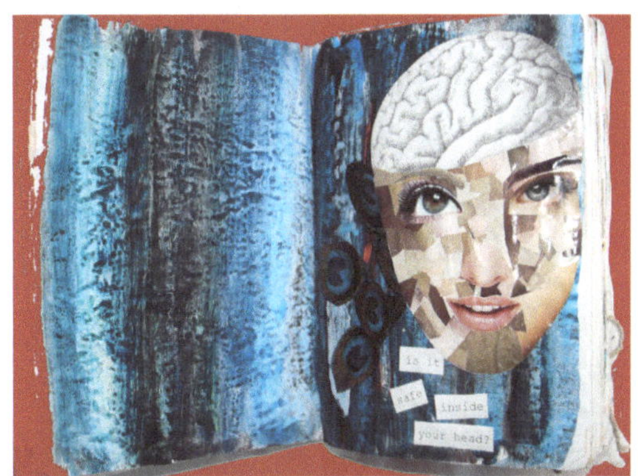

Your Way

Do you have a sketchbook? Has Taylor inspired you to start one? Many artists keep a sketchbook that they can bring everywhere they go. Others bring their experiences home to their sketchbooks. Either way, keeping a sketchbook is a marvelous way to make sure you always have a place to make a quick drawing, jot down an observation, or capture an idea that you don't want to forget. You can make your own sketchbook by folding paper or cutting pages and stapling or fastening them together. If you plan to carry it with you, be sure it's not too big, so it can fit into a pocket or a bag.

Your sketchbook can be as complex as Taylor's or you can keep it very simple. To spark your creativity you may consider preparing some of the pages by applying a watercolor wash or prepping the surface with lines, splotches or collages before you actually sketch. Challenge yourself by trying to do a drawing every day for a week, or even longer. Pick your favorite and make a larger, more developed piece from your original sketch.

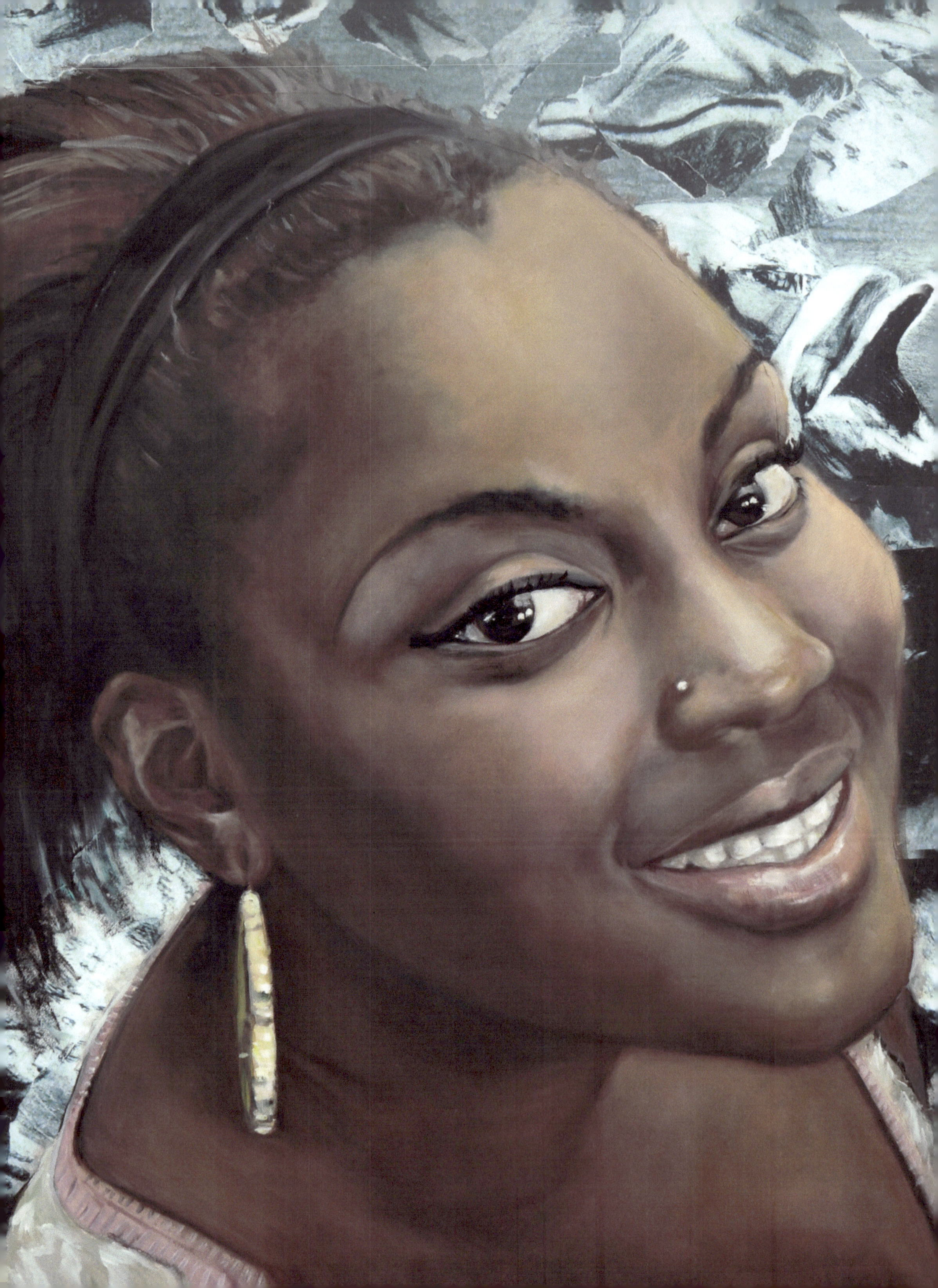

Portraits

When I was young, I saw my brother doing art so I wanted to draw like him, but everyone said my art was abstract. So I kept drawing, thinking I would get to his level. As I turned thirteen, I just started doing it for fun.

A few years ago I was getting into trouble. When I felt like doing something stupid, I would draw instead.

I'm very impatient so I tend to rush through things, but even so I'm always impressed by how it turns out.

I just keep drawing because it's something I'm good at.

-Jaime

Jaime's portraits are much more than likenesses of people. She instills each one with mood and attitude, adding a vitality that makes them come alive.

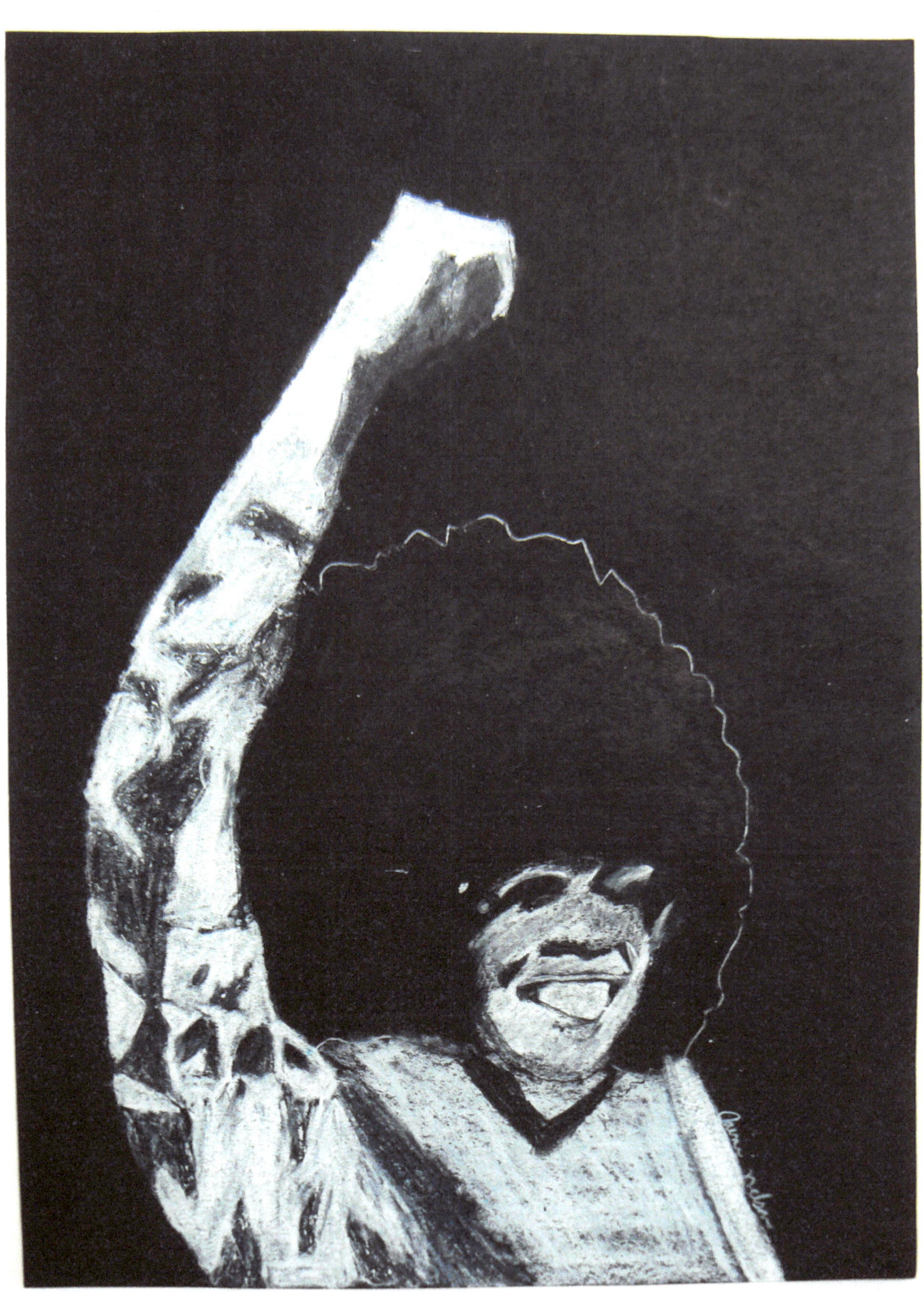

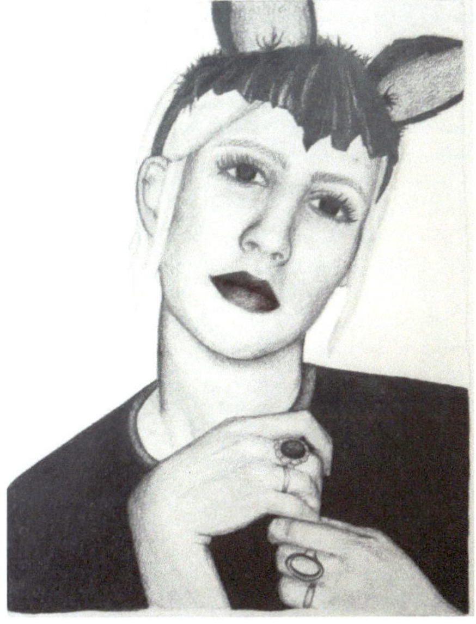

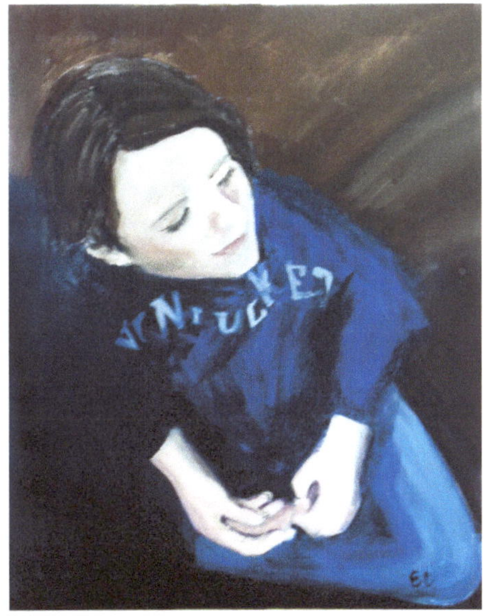

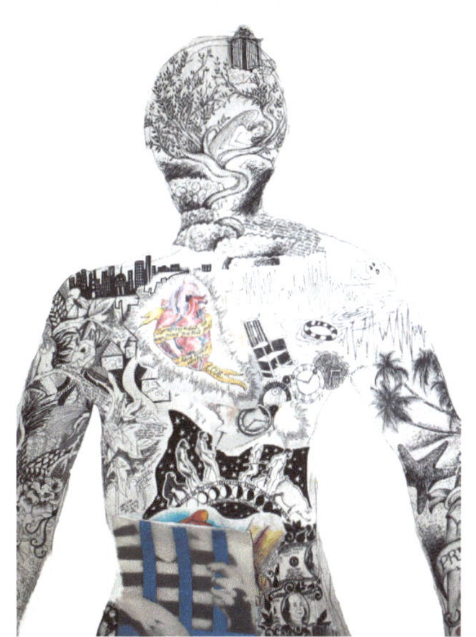

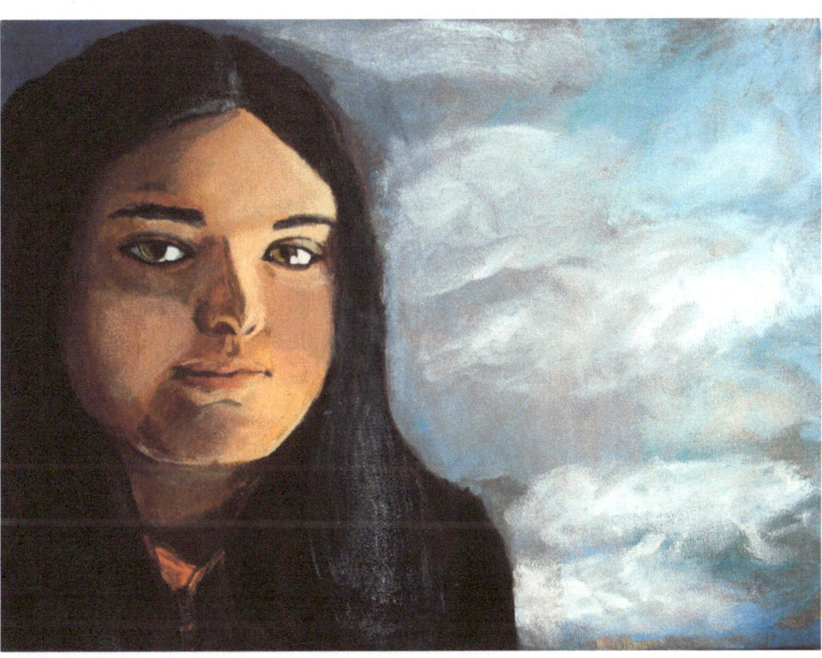

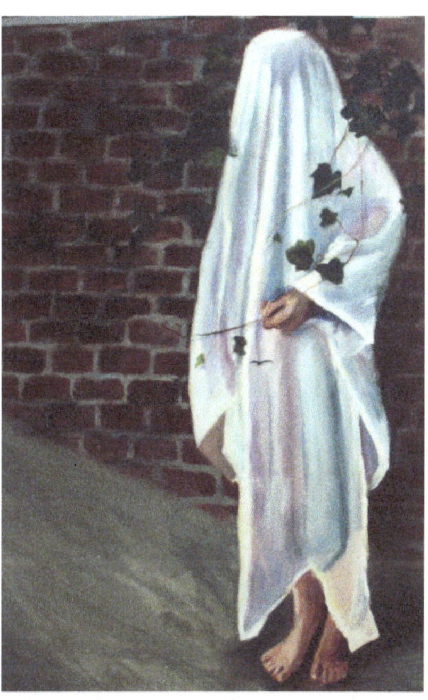

Your Way

Can you create a portrait without showing a person? How can you represent them in another way? Perhaps you might try reproducing the features of your subject as accurately as you can, and then create an abstract portrait of the same person. Which one captures the attitude and personality of the person better?

About Jaime pg 72

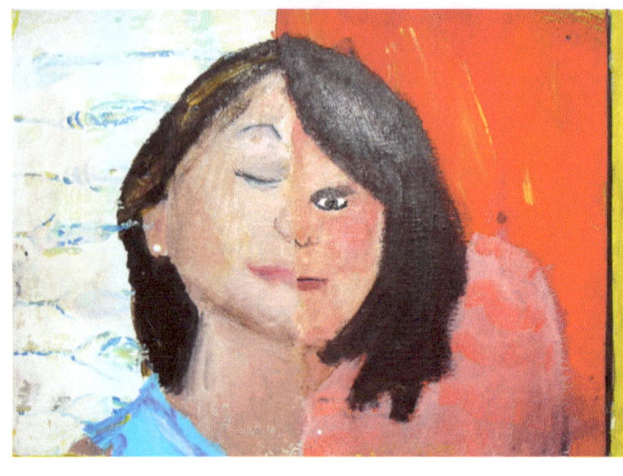
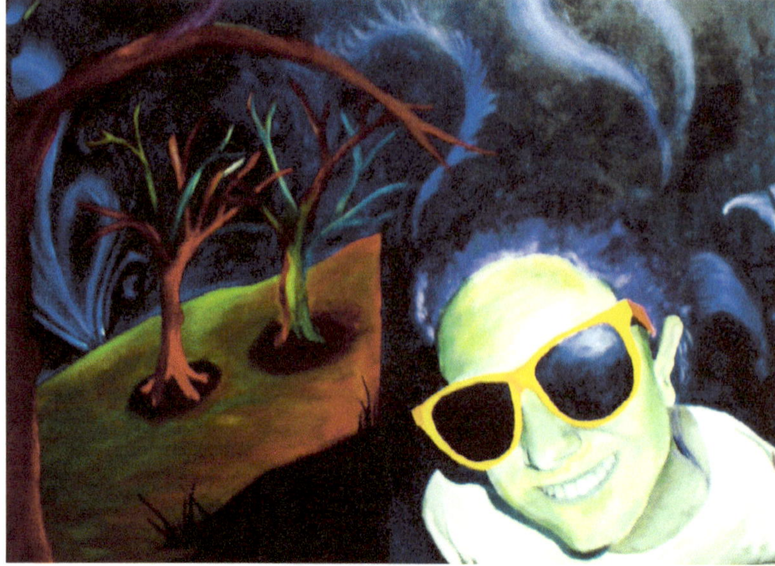
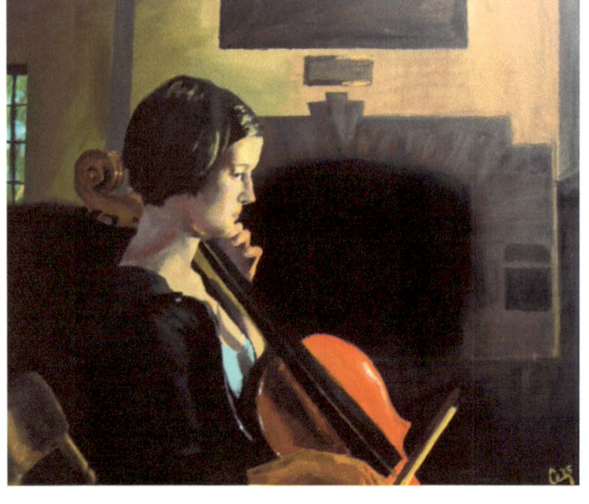
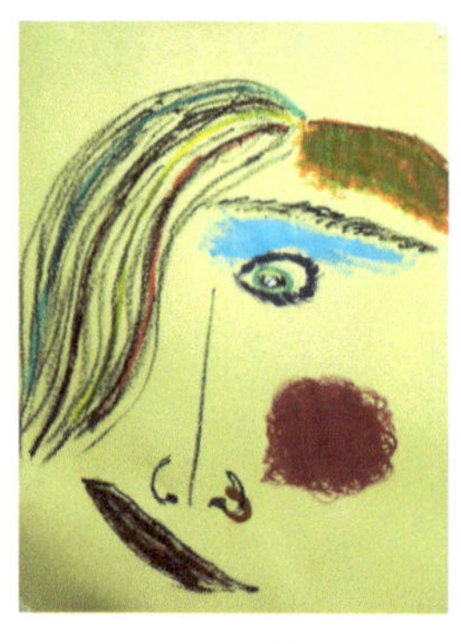
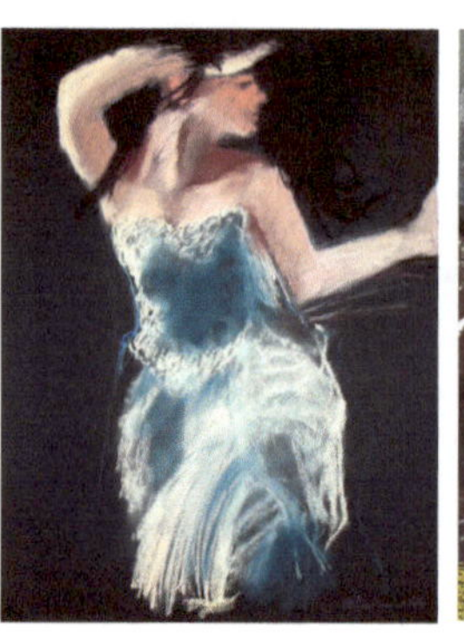
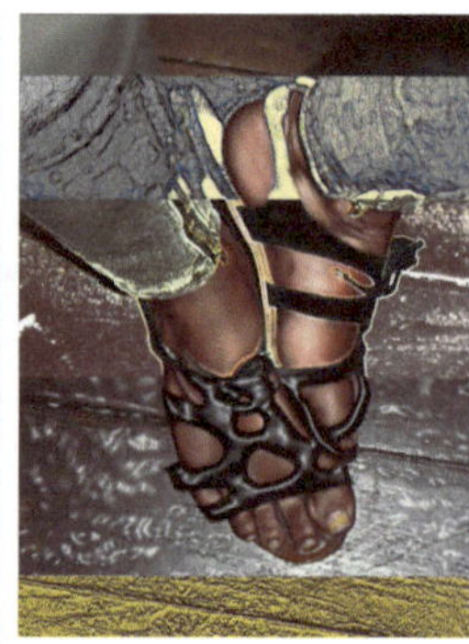
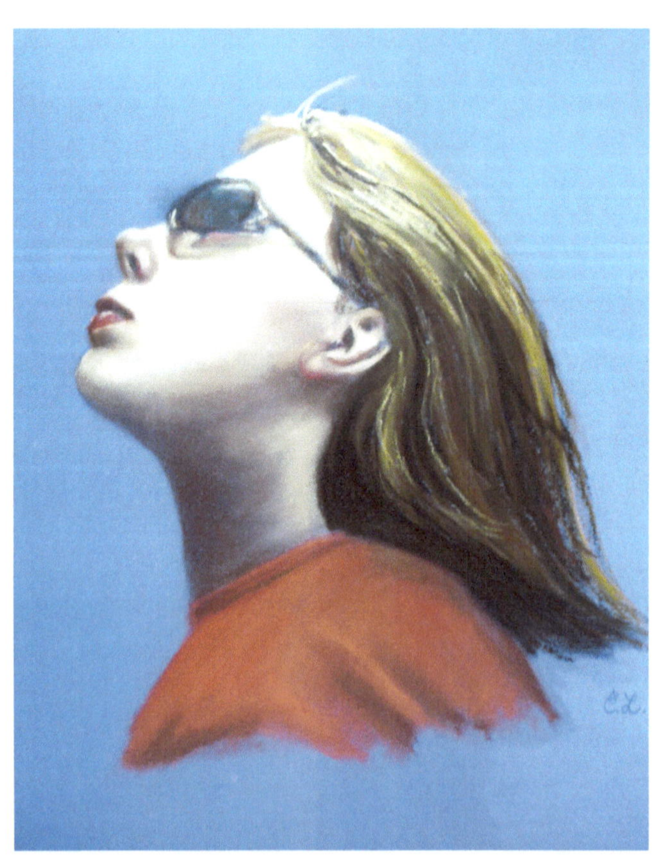
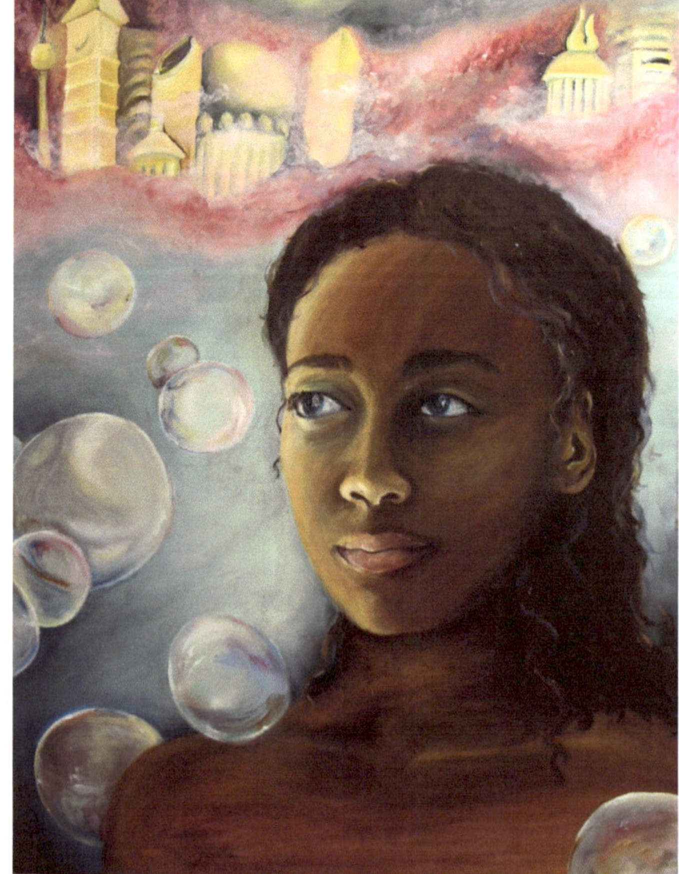

Art Credits & Titles

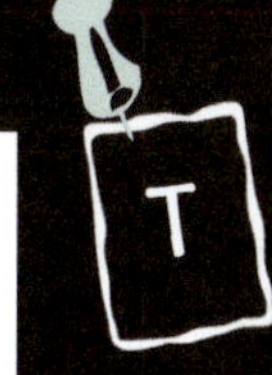

All images referenced from left to right, down the page.

All Front Cover Art:
Elena Caravela, Oil Portraits & Mixed Media
Back Cover:
Jessica, *Untitled*, Collage
Hayley, *Untitled*, Acrylic
Elizabeth C, *Still Life with Purse*, Pastel
Cali, *Tortured Fruit*, Acrylic
Brianna, *Earth's Accomplishments*, Graphite
Serena, *Untitled*, Marker
Audrey, *Timmy the Turtle*, Pastel
Naomi, *Not Me*, Acrylic
Emily, *Close-Up in Blue*, Acrylic
Kerri, *Lonely*, Graphite
Front Gallery Page:
Ali, *Converse*, Pastel
Leah, *Hot Tea*, Mixed Media
Annie, *Untitled*, Graphite
Samantha, *Untitled*, Acrylic
Elizabeth L, *Flies*, Digital
Cali, *Untitled*, Acrylic
Taylor, *Caps & Glass*, Hub Caps & Lucite
Taylor, *Blue Shoes*, pastel
Title Gallery Page:
Kate, *Yogurt Brushes*, Acrylic
Katie, *Keith & Sarah*, Acrylic
Ali, *Self-Portrait*, Acrylic
Hayley, *Untitled*, Conte Crayon
YOUR ART!
Emily, *Self-Portrait*, Acrylic
Annie S, *Rooster*, Pastel
Grace, *Untitled*, Acrylic
Audrey, *My Hand*, Acrylic
Title Page:
Katie, *Elena*, Acrylic
Dedication Page:
Elena, *Taylor*, Oil
My World Galleries:
Katie, *9/11 Dust & Paper Cloud*, Acrylic
Katie, *9/11 McDonalds*, Acrylic
Katie, *9/11 Tom's Homecoming*, Acrylic
Katie, *9/11 Iron Man*, Acrylic
Katie, *My Cousin's Wedding, Scott & Becky*, Acrylic
Ellie, *Fourth of July*, Acrylic
Emma, *Veneer*, Mixed Media
Samantha, *Swan Lake*, Watercolor
Multipurpose Galleries:
Lara, *Untitled*, Painted Ceramic
Taylor, *Watch Your Step*, Mixed Media Digital
Kate, *Urban Cowgirl*, Collage
Martha, *Salt & Pepper*, Clay
Imagination Galleries:
Serena, *Dragon*, Tempera
Serena, *Untitled*, Mixed Media
Leah, *Shadow Creatures*, Cut Paper
Grace, *Nightmare*, Acrylic
Katie, *Cow & Bubble Troubles*, Acrylic
Leah, *Hathi the Elephant*, Mixed Media Puppetry
The Artist Inside Galleries:
Ayanna, *Untitled*, Tempera
Emma, *Disparity*, Graphite
Amanda, *My Cup*, Acrylic
Anna, *Gum Lover*, Opaque Watercolor
Meghan, *Huck*, Oil Stick
Showcasing Galleries:
Claire, *The Reader*, Watercolor
Tara, *Untitled*, Acrylic
Jennie, *Untitled*, Oil
Samantha, *October Apples*, Acrylic
Light and Dark Galleries:
Cynthia, *Cathedral*, Oil
Katherine, *Light Study*, Oil
Aurelia, *Origins*, Pastel
Jessica, *Untitled*, Acrylic
Taylor, *Nuru*, Graphite
Secret Codes & Symbols Galleries:
Dianne, *The City*, Acrylic
Serena, *Untitled*, Acrylic
Audrey, *The City*, Acrylic
Zoe, *Spirals*, Acrylic
Jessica, *Untitled*, Fumage & Mixed Media
Design Galleries:
Elizabeth, *The Scarlet Letter*, Digital and Embroidery Thread
Taylor, *Bartholomew and the Oobleck*, Mixed Media
Kate, *Hattie Blue Sky*, Opaque Watercolor
Leah, *Legend of the Raven God King*, Photography
Leah, *Red Riding Hood*, Photography & Mixed Media
Leah, *Guide to Egyptian Gods & Goddesses*, Mixed Media
Audrey, *Candy Floss*, Mixed Media
Discovery Galleries:
Katherine, *Rhododendron Leaves 2*, Leaves, Metallic Marker & Straight Pins
Katherine, *Untitled (Pine & Bark Fragments)*, Pine & Bark Fragments
Kate, *Apeel Tree*, Apple
Ali, *Seagulls*, Shells
Audrey, *Bungaloo Turtle*, Cotton & Rocks
Emotions Galleries:
Ali, *Anxiety*, Mixed Media
Ali, *Untitled*, Acrylic
Aurelia, *Interconnection*, Watercolor
Aurelia, *Mrs. M*, Mixed Media
Emma, *Energy*, Acrylic
Naomi, *Ranya*, Pastel
Elizabeth L, *Arabesque*, Oil Sticks
Experimenting Galleries:
Leah, *Arnolfini Portrait Ala 1970s*, Mixed Media Collage
Kate, *Jazz Cafe*, Mixed Media
Emma, *Cloud*, Mixed Media
Taylor, *Time*, Collage
Leah, *Subterranean Dragon*, Traditional & Digital Collage
The True You Galleries:
Rachel, *Self-Portrait*, Acrylic
Amanda, *In My Head*, Acrylic
Audrey, *My Twisted Mind*, Acrylic
Kate, *Daydream*, Acrylic
Martha, *Self-Portrait*, Clay & Glaze
Blending Interests Galleries:
Tara, *The Coral Breath*, Pastel
Tara, *Thirteen Years*, Acrylic
Betsy, *Violin & Cat*, Conte Crayon
Hayley, *Untitled*, Mixed Media
Audrey, *The Swimmer*, Acrylic
All Sketchbook Art:
All by Taylor:
Sketchbook Cover II, Mixed Media
Sketchbook Page: Idealism, Mixed Media
Sketchbook Page: Untitled
Sketchbook Page: Stitches & Scars
Sketchbook Page: Untitled
Sketchbook Page: Mad World
Portraits Galleries:
Jaime, *Angela*, Charcoal
Annie, *Untitled*, Graphite
Elizabeth L, *Self-Portrait*, Acrylic
Taylor, *An Interview with a Reformed Rake -or- Looking Through a Glass Onion*, Mixed Media
Amanda, *Self-Portrait*, Acrylic
Katherine, *Trapped in 9/11*, Acrylic
Kate & Audrey, *Opposites Attract*, Acrylic
Katherine, *self portrait (green face) 2002*, Acrylic
Cynthia, *Alison*, Acrylic
Amanda, *Made to Impress*, Oil Pastel
Ali, *Untitled*, Pastel
Emma, *Feet*, Photography & Digital
Elizabeth L, *Hayley*, Pastel
Taylor, *Rachel*, Oil
Sketches Page:
Elena, *Dab*, Pastel
Back Gallery Page:
Elizabeth, *Recluse*, Pastel
Kim, *Untitled*, Acrylic
Rachel, *Dust Kitty*, Digital Painting
MacKenzie, *Dreaded Tea Kettle*, Charcoal
Taylor, *Chasing Birds*, Mixed Media
Naomi, *Fans*, Prismacolor
Claudia, *A Night Out*, Charcoal
Aurelia, *Gateway to Hell*, Photography
Annie, *Untitled*, Prismacolor
Betsy, *Sunset Beach*, Acrylic
Elizabeth L, *Flowers*, Pastel
Leah, *Self-Portrait*, Acrylic

Sketches

Katie: My World

"Fearless" is the first word that comes to mind when I think of Katie. Her infectious laugh and exuberance were rarely dampened by the additional time and hard work she had to put in at school. Her dyslexia isn't a secret nor a problem. Katie's different way of learning is simply another facet of her warm, hilarious, take-no-prisoners personality. I think that learning differently even offers Katie a gift—a brain that is just different enough to construct a unique window on the world.

Always ready to dive into a new project, Katie thrives on big canvases and bold ideas. At times watching her work was like sitting in the front row of a one-person improv performance. Katie's face twisted from one expression to the next while she remarked on any number of topics, from food to friends to her fascination with cows (the subject of quite a few of her paintings). Any setback she encountered was met with a vocal complaint followed by a smile. Katie's rewards are her accomplishments. No matter how much work she takes on, Katie somehow finds energy to spare for the people around her.

A big part of Katie's world is her family and friends. In the artwork included here, she depicts two dramatically different but palpably life-changing events: the 9/11 attack on the Twin Towers, made more personal for her because her father was working near the Towers that day, and a celebratory depiction of her cousin's wedding. As much as these two works contrast in tone, color, and composition, they're both examples of Katie creating art to interpret and respond to the world around her.

In her first semester of college, Katie was the only freshman whose work was included in a high-profile art exhibit at her school. I'm sure that being included in the show reinforced Katie's belief in herself as a creative and talented individual. Katie later graduated with honors, not only in her art major but in her overall coursework as well. I can't think of Katie without breaking into a smile almost as generous as hers, an impulse I share with everyone who knows her. You can imagine how honored I felt when Katie presented a giant portrait she painted of me, rendered in colors as bright as her personality. That painting lives in my home, hung in a place where I can soak up a little bit of Katie's dynamic energy whenever I need it.

Lara: Multipurpose

"I am full of art," says Lara. Anyone who knows her understands exactly what she means. Her ability to recognize magic in everyday objects is matched by her gift for communicating visually. While Lara may agree with the phrase "a picture is worth a thousand words," her creativity is rarely contained by two dimensions, let alone one or two forms of visual expression. She often works in clay creating three-dimensional pieces with two-dimensional embellishments.

Quiet and thoughtful by nature, Lara is instantly transformed when she enters the studio. The freedom and contentment she feels is clearly evident when she is creating art. It is obvious in the vivid colors and variety of materials she chooses. What impresses me most about Lara is the way she is able to redefine our judgments. Lara's repurposing of a teapot is just one example. After she has taken this common object and remade it, one wonders if the result is still a vessel for pouring tea or a sculpture to be appreciated as art. As she applies her artistic vision to everyday experience, Lara challenges our notions about how objects (and even people) are categorized and judged. While some of us often struggle to find the right words to express ourselves, Lara's gift enables her to visualize her thoughts and translate them directly into pictures. This ability to convey emotions and ideas through images has already served her well as the illustrator of two published books, with yet another in progress. These are certainly achievements to be proud of, but Lara derives an even greater sense of satisfaction from the process of communicating through her art. With her talent for finding inspiration in unexpected places, I'm confident that Lara will forever be "full of art".

Serena: Imagination

Serena is the granddaughter of one of my mother's good friends. That's how I became aware of Serena's insatiable urge to draw. When I actually saw a few of Serena's whimsical and vibrant creations for myself, it was evident that Serena's work belonged in this book. Later I was fortunate to get to know Serena a little, and was left with the impression of a thoughtful and focused girl with a keen and inventive way of thinking.

At first glance you might not expect such a vivid imagination to lie behind Serena's composed and confident demeanor. But as you get to know Serena, her sense of playfulness begins to come through. Serena's self-discipline is clear from the fact that she's an excellent student and tackles her schoolwork and musical study with intensity. Her analytical approach is evident in how she questions instructions and suggestions, always in an incisive yet respectful way. Art is Serena's outlet for the world of her dreams, rendered with characteristic care but colored by imagination.

The characters Serena creates are joyous, vibrant creatures who aren't above a bit of mischief. They seem to be the sort of companions Serena would be happy to have along on a voyage to a magical realm where they are free to frolic or even misbehave. The only thing for sure in this land of imagination is that Serena is in charge.

Ayanna: The Artist Inside

Sparkly eyes and on the go, those are the first things you can't help noticing about Ayanna. She also has a lot of interesting things to say, and she isn't shy about expressing herself, in words or in art. I imagine that her confidence, energy and enthusiasm have helped her excel in many activities, and she brings those qualities to her general approach to life. I was fortunate to connect with Ayanna through Sisterhood Agenda Magazine, a publication devoted to empowering the self-development of African American women and girls. When I contacted the founder of its parent organization and told her about this book, she graciously introduced me to Ayanna's artwork. It was wonderful to discover such a very young person who is so beautifully self-possessed. Ayanna exudes an unshakable belief in herself and in her identity. Part of that identity is being an artist.

A naturally perceptive girl, Ayanna is able to make connections between her own thoughts and feelings and what she sees in the world. She notices qualities in common objects and familiar scenes that other people might easily overlook. She has the ability to view the commonplace in new ways, by adjusting light, color and point of view. Combining her observations with shades of meaning she draws from within, she finds joy in making art and in the varied perspectives and opportunities it gives her. Ayanna knows she's an artist and keeps herself open to the creative possibilities around her, never allowing false modesty to disguise her strength or cloud her vision. With such drive and determination to nurture her innate creative spirit, I know that both her faith in herself and her identity as an artist will remain strong throughout her life.

Claire: Showcasing

Claire welcomes the opportunity to share her art! I learned about Claire's work through her art teacher, who happened to be related to a good friend of mine. When she heard about my book, Claire's teacher didn't hesitate to recommend her as an artist I should consider including. Once I received a plump oversized envelope in the mail containing Claire's work, I readily agreed. With the help of photographs selected by her mother and Claire's written responses to some of the questions I'd sent to her, a portrait of this talented young artist soon came together. I could tell that Claire was intelligent, confident, and dedicated to her art. I was struck by her interest in history and humanity, particularly in how our actions affect the lives of others.

Claire is very clear about the fact that she is indeed an artist, and she takes great satisfaction in displaying her work. When told by her teacher that her class would be participating in a contest sponsored by the Robert Russa Moton Museum for Civil Rights Education, Claire promptly began working on her entry. The Moton Museum is dedicated to preserving the history of civil rights in education, commemorating a student-led strike held in 1951 at the then-segregated high school. After learning about the school and meeting some of the brave people who protested, Claire decided to create a piece showing the fruits of their efforts. Her work is a painting depicting children of many races sitting happily together on a school bus. She won first prize and her piece was displayed in the Moton Museum!

Naturally, Claire felt good to know that her art was seen as important. Her concept, skill and hard work had been acknowledged. But even if she had not won, Claire would not have lost confidence in her abilities. With encouragement from her family and the respect of her teachers and friends, Claire has a solid base of support. She knows that sometimes it takes a long time to achieve recognition as an artist, but that she could not have won first prize without the courage and confidence to put her work forward. While Claire finds it tremendously rewarding that others appreciate her art, I'm sure that she will continue to challenge herself artistically. She can't help it. She's an artist.

Cynthia: Light and Dark

Anime very much influenced the young, flaxen haired Cynthia. Even at seven, Cynthia could draw very well, but she credits Anime as the inspiration to first pick up a pencil. As Cynthia's art instructor, I wanted her to discover her own distinctive way of making art. So as the stylized Anime proportions diminished in her work, Cynthia began to use her own eyes, brain, and heart to interpret her subjects. Soon she was able to capture what she saw and chose to depict in accurate but artful detail.

Cynthia is still enchanted by all things Japanese but she is much more open to all sorts of other influences as well. Her hair color has reflected every richness of red hue I can imagine and her interests now include biology, specifically the study of cuttlefish. I imagine that's not a coincidence since the cuttlefish has the ability to camouflage itself by instantly changing its skin color. Not that Cynthia much cares to blend in. She's independent and confident. It's the cuttlefish's mechanism that registers changes in its environment that strikes me as significant for Cynthia. This is evident in the color values and the spectrum of light and dark in Cynthia's featured work.

It would be fair to say that Cynthia's art reflects her nature, since she could be described as a study in contrasts. She is an excellent draftsperson. Her drawings from the microscope are accurate but also very beautiful works of art. She is an avid rock climber and an indie fashion icon. She can appreciate a good structured exercise but will always remain a free thinker. As this book goes to press, Cynthia is about to graduate college with a degree in biology. I know that her discerning intelligence, crooked smile, love for science and all styles of art will forever endear her to those who know her, myself especially. I also know that these characteristics will prove invaluable throughout her career and her life.

Dianne: Secret Codes and Symbols

Good at so many things, it's difficult to tease apart all of Dianne's many talents. She is a lovely bundle of compassion, razor-sharp intelligence, good humor, and enthusiasm. I'm trying not to gush because Dianne is my niece. I feel justified in my braggy assessment, however, because Dianne's teachers have described her in much the same way. Dianne truly has the world by the tail, yet like everyone else she sometimes feels the need to turn inward and keep some things private.

Dianne was just over six years old when she worked on the piece featured here. She was visiting for the day, and much to my delight, she wanted to paint in my studio. Dianne is a book hound, so before any painting commenced we browsed my collection of art books. She was taken with the colorful abstracts of Miro and Kandinsky, and we talked about the joy and underlying mysteries of their work. Inspired by the paintings, Dianne wove a detailed story about what their shapes and colors meant to her. I felt as though I was sharing an afternoon with a really creative young philosopher. I supplied materials and Dianne painted, all the while explaining her methods and supplying clues to her story, creating her own personal symbols with each brushstroke.

This coding approach to making art works well for Dianne. When her dog Storm passed away she drew pictures and felt a bit better, but she did not want to share those pictures with everybody. It was important for her to transform her feelings into images, but also to keep them private. She found comfort in creating art that spoke to her alone. But she did not want to feel she had to hide her work. The symbols and code method satisfied Dianne's need for privacy and self-expression without the need for secrecy.

At the time of this writing Dianne is eleven years old, and while her interest in art and symbol-making has continued, she has become more collaborative, working with her close friends to create a series of characters and stories, always with accompanying illustrations. Her interests in theatre and figure skating have brought elements of drama, music and dance to her growing palette of self-expression. All of these things have contributed to the development of Dianne's unique creative language. She is still judicious in choosing what to share and what to save for herself. But Dianne knows she will always have a personal space to express her most private fears and feelings.

Elizabeth: Design

"Elizabeth" and "design" have become synonymous to me—I can't think of one without the other. Through grades K-12, Elizabeth could not hand in a piece of schoolwork without embellishing it first, framing the paper with patterns and drawings. It would be an understatement to say that her teachers failed to be impressed, but that was because they didn't understand Elizabeth's need to exorcise her design demons! In the studio, her fascination with pure design was impossible to ignore. As a little girl, Elizabeth even covered herself in swirls, patterns, and colors, sometimes spending hours painting intricate patterns on her hand (often when she was supposed to be working on another project). Her "hand paintings" were so beautiful, however, that I insisted on taking digital photos and keeping them as part of Elizabeth's early portfolio. I still have the files.

Her ability to put other people at ease with her poise and conversation skills has always been part of Elizabeth's winning personality. To put it simply, she is a marvelous communicator. Her love of drawing and painting is strong, but is exceeded by her hunger to understand, condense, and solidify her subject through the visual messages of design. She knows that as important as it is to explore her own insights and bring her unique approach to her projects, her designs will succeed only if they provoke feeling and understanding in her audience.

Elizabeth will readily admit that academics were never her strong suit, but when she won a scholarship to art school she excelled, devouring her coursework. Soon after graduation she was offered a position as a junior art director (with a design organization so well known that it qualifies as a household name). Today, everyone who knows Elizabeth is duly impressed. I'm so very proud to have been a part of her creative journey. Success could not have come to a more deserving artist.

Katherine: Discovery

Katherine is able to really "see" a leaf, a stone, or a person without automatic classification. She has the rare ability to observe without preconceptions, not judging but allowing the person or object to define itself. Coupled with her gift is a capacity to bring out the beauty in what she sees, not by idealizing it but by directing our attention to its essence. What Katherine is able to do is hard to describe, but that's as it should be. When we open ourselves to her art we understand.

Katherine doesn't talk much about her observations, but she seems to absorb everything. She is keenly aware of the people around her, and her insights into their moods and feelings have made her a quiet leader. She is not a wishful thinker, but when she perceives threatened beauty she doesn't hesitate to step in and do what she can to nurture it through her art and her actions. It is important to Katherine to use her creativity to wake us up, open our eyes and nudge us in a positive direction.

A fine arts major in college, Katherine looked for ways to apply her talents to practical goals. She organized group projects and exhibits, designed costumes for plays, and assisted her peers and professors with their work. In the midst of all these activities, Katherine continued to gather, reclaim and revitalize objects in the development of her own art, creating some truly extraordinary pieces. Intent on promoting positive change, Katherine designed a program to teach art to at-risk teens in a county detention center, bringing fresh insight into the lives of her students.

Katherine continues to devote herself to the teaching program she developed and also works as an exhibit coordinator in a thriving community arts center. Somehow she manages to work tirelessly at both, and plans to expand her teaching efforts to reach more children and adults. Before you assume that Katherine is all work and no fun, you should know that she is also an amazing belly dancer! I admire everything about Katherine and I remain in awe of her talents.

Ali: Emotions

We all struggle with them, and rejoice in them. We all express them differently. Our emotions can rule us or we can learn how to live well with them. For Ali making art is a way to direct and express emotion. But this realization took some time for Ali to understand. She was quite young when she began taking art classes, and her first concerns were learning about materials and developing skills. However, as she became more comfortable in the studio, her compassionate nature began to find its way into her work. It was inevitable because Ali shines with a warmth and empathy that you can see in her eyes. I have always been impressed with how considerate and tolerant she is, qualities that can be present only when one is sensitive to her own feelings.

As she grew, Ali learned how different emotions could be conveyed through colors, textures, and line, establishing a visual vocabulary that allowed her to express many different moods. With practice, creating art that reflected what she was feeling became more and more intuitive. As Ali's artistic confidence grew she knew that she could excel in other areas as well.

With her keen interest in people and expressing emotion, it's no surprise that Ali is fascinated by the study of the mind. Psychology is her major in college, supported by a minor in art. This combination enables her to remain sensitive to others while allowing her to relieve and express her own emotions in a creative way. Ali understands that the act of making art can be extremely powerful and rewarding, both in the process and the pride the artist takes in her finished work. She is even considering courses in art therapy.

I feel very fortunate to know Ali. She brings a heartfelt hug and lots of good humor wherever she goes. I'm also pleased that Ali will soon be able to counsel others. She's well equipped with her intensive study and with the tools of her artistic insight.

Leah: Experimenting

It didn't take more that a couple of hours for me to understand that Leah was born to be a visual artist. I met her when she was seven years old. She was quiet, sweet, and a bit shy, preferring to allow the world in a little at a time. She was cautious with her drawing but she was also determined to improve her skills. As her confidence grew so did her sense of adventure.

Leah is still as sweet, loyal and patient as she was then, but some things have changed. Today if you were to meet Leah you'd first notice her clothes—crazy sneakers, stripes and bold colors matching her wild curls. She has an offbeat sense of humor and appreciates all things retro. Leah loves music and has a wonderful voice, but would rather be part of a band than a solo act. She literally jumps at the chance to try new ways of working, revealing her sense of whimsy in everything she creates.

Leah works in many different types of media, constantly amazing me with how well she is able to manipulate each one. While the dedication she showed to practicing her drawing and painting when she was very young has served her well, Leah's willingness to experiment has allowed her and her talent to blossom.

Judging by the recognition she has already received, her college professors are as impressed with her creative range as I am. Leah has already written and illustrated two children's books, produced her own short films, and pursued her love of puppetry to design and build a menagerie of weirdly wonderful characters.

It's been such a pleasure to watch Leah grow into a loving, confident, and exciting young woman and artist. I suspect that many more people will know the wide range and quality of her work before too long. You already know what she can do to help transform a ho-hum book into one I hope you find exciting. Yes, I mean THIS book. Couldn't have done it without her.

Rachel: The True You

Quirky, funny, and clever, Rachel is her own person, as articulate in her visual art as she is with words. Being creative comes naturally to her, though she is not aware of what a truly wonderful gift that is. For many girls the social pressure to narrowly conform—to dress and behave only in one accepted way—terribly inhibits their personalities and creativity. This mode of operation is not for Rachel. Rachel can't help but BE Rachel. Her lanky grace compliments her witty and charming personality. And it seems that girls who get to know Rachel forget "the rules" and really enjoy her sophisticated humor and overall nonconformity.

Rachel has always been comfortable with exploring her imagination and developing a clear vision to express her art. If Rachel has a challenge it is to stay focused and see her projects through to a finished state. That's no easy task with a mind constantly dreaming up new concepts.

Rachel enjoys writing, digital artwork and making art with traditional materials. The medium of cartooning, however, is a natural one for Rachel, allowing her to illustrate more ideas in a single project and to tell whole stories in her drawings. She often uses fantastic or surrealistic settings to reveal a deeper truth. Rachel's greatest motivation to create art is to communicate the images and thoughts in her head and her featured piece represents a straightforward way of doing just that.

Rachel's talent lies in the ability to truly be herself. I look forward to bragging that I knew Rachel before she was famous and just learning how to express herself through art.

Tara: Blending Interests

Tara smiles with her entire being. At first glance, she appears to be a light hearted and serene person. That's an accurate impression, but what you may not immediately suspect is the depth and scope of her varied interests. For evidence of that, you need only look at her artwork. Tara's creations depict her love of family, animals, friends, and science. Pastels are her favorite medium, because in her hands they blend together as naturally as Tara's interests. Her curiosity about the world has fueled her love of travel and her interest in how things work. Tara looks to science for answers to some of her questions.

One reason Tara is able to become engaged so wholeheartedly in so many pursuits is that she has no time for pretense or vanity. She is a sincere and genuine person and her unassuming attitude radiates a special charm. Tara has a gift for finding common ground with whomever she meets. She takes great pleasure in making art that brings joy to others. In turn, she finds joy in the creative process.

It seems to me that Tara has always been able to define what is important to her, and has always been willing to work tirelessly at what she loves. Her refusal to limit herself to a narrow field of pursuits has made her an interesting and well-rounded person. Her art is a tribute to the lovely elements that come together to form Tara. Under her tranquil exterior, Tara's passions burn brightly.

Taylor: Sketchbook

A wise old soul from a young age, in some ways Taylor has always seemed like a little grown-up. By the time she shares an idea, it's obvious that Taylor has already considered and analyzed it. You can tell by the way she speaks, with a matter-of-fact tone that's confident but never arrogant, infused with her wry sense of humor. Her strategy is the same when it comes to her art: take time for a piece to germinate, then develop and organize it, and finally, commit to it!

An invaluable tool in Taylor's process is her sketchbook. Taylor was about sixteen when she repurposed an ordinary composition book as her diary and sketchbook. She jotted down her thoughts, intently writing and drawing whatever she was thinking and feeling. Before long that sketchbook was bursting, so Taylor invented a new book capable of containing work that represented the full range of her artistry. With her distinctive brand of insight and heart, Taylor created an ingenious sketchbook out of a cake mix box. It is an expandable volume that can accommodate unexpected three-dimensional objects, collages, and paper sculptures along with her fantastic two-dimensional work. Her cake box containers are genius. For Taylor they serve as a personal diary and a birthing place for all sorts of finished work.

In Taylor's books you can discover her fascination with cars, her tattoo designs, her poetry, her loves, her keen interest in biology, her heartbreaks and the assorted inspirations she's picked up from her many travels. In all, you will find a profile of an astute observer, a thinker, and a sensitive soul. Her sketchbooks hold the mementos from all sorts of journeys.

Because Taylor is so caring and giving, she's allowed me to share these intimate and extraordinary sketchbooks with you. Taylor, you are amazing.

Jaime: Portraits

I am grateful that working on this book has brought me the opportunity to learn of so many talented young artists. As I discussed my plans for the book with my friends, and as word traveled, many of them told me they knew (or knew of) young women with a deeply rooted love of drawing or painting. Jaime came to my attention that way—her art teacher was her enthusiastic supporter. When I saw Jaime's work, I knew that I had to include her in this book.

Jaime's interest in art began by watching her older brother draw. Jaime became inspired to improve her own skills. She found that the more she learned, the more she enjoyed making art. Jaime feels a well-deserved pride in her artistic accomplishments, and that feeling helps her deal with many of the challenges most teenagers have to face. Art is a positive outlet for her, a channel for her energy. With every piece Jaime completes, she grows as an artist and as a young woman. Each creative achievement reinforces her self-respect.

I think Jaime's specialty is painting portraits. She does a marvelous job of depicting her subjects' unique character. But there is also a part of Jaime in each piece as well. Her sense of self-assurance, her joy, satisfaction, concentration, and expectation. As a portrait painter myself, I know that in every portrait there is a reflection of the artist. I can see Jaime's beauty in her featured piece.

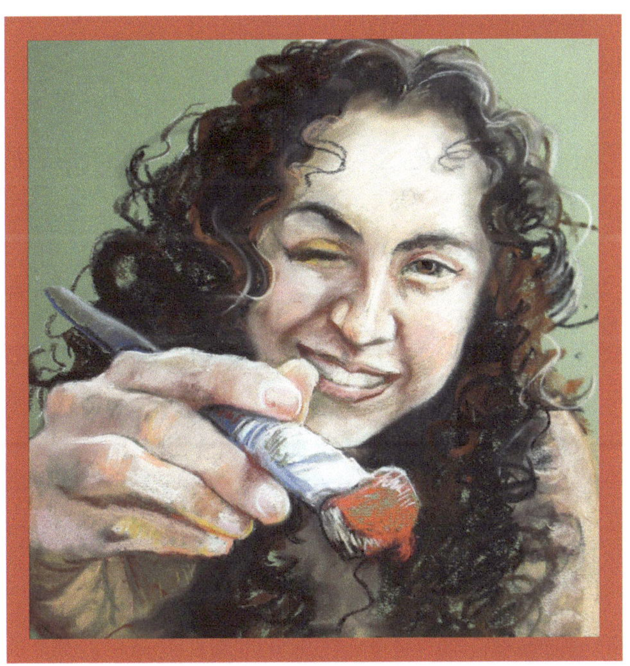

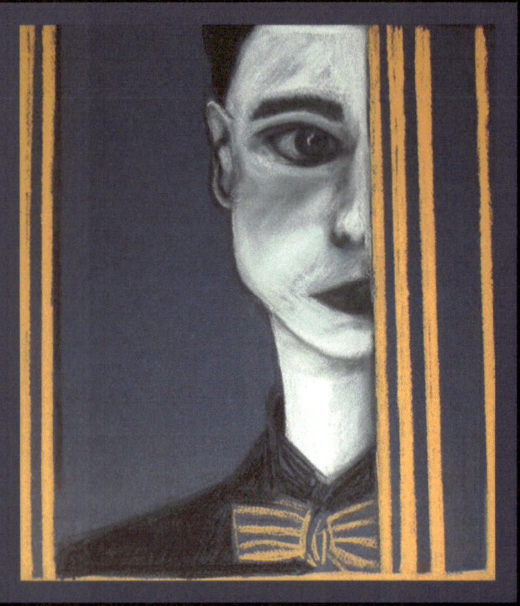

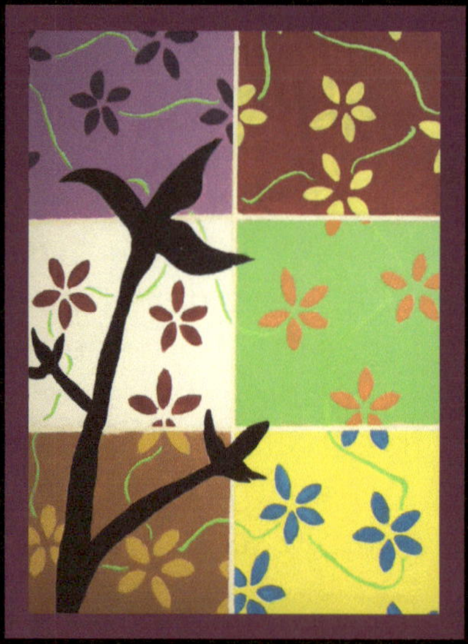

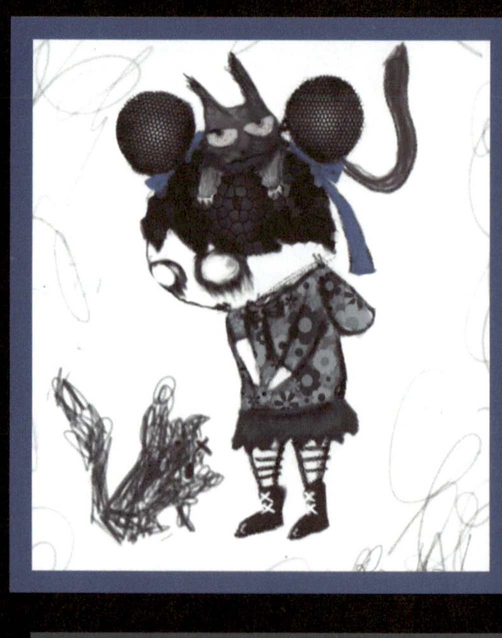

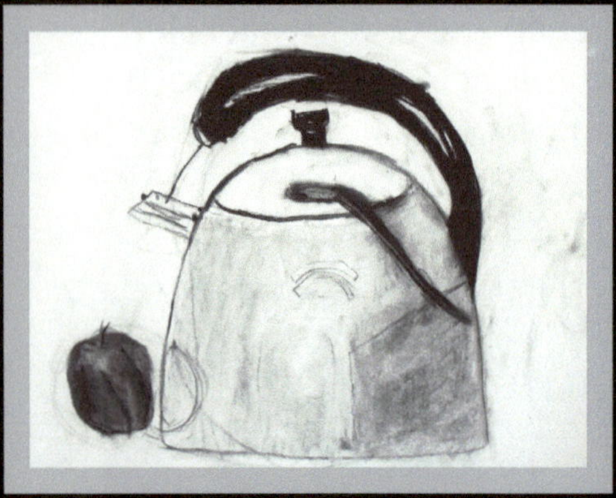

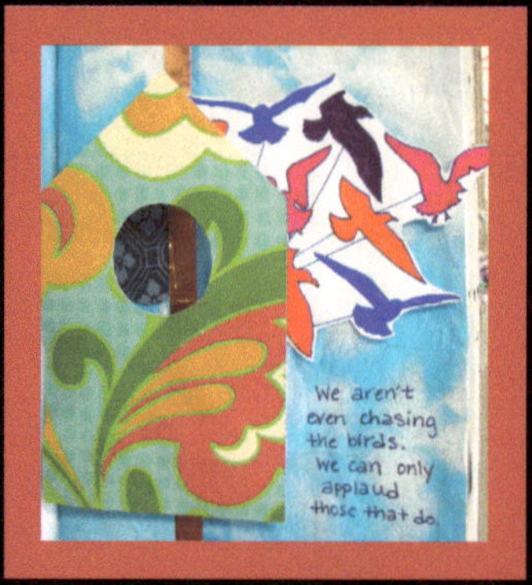

We aren't
even chasing
the birds.
We can only
applaud
those that do.

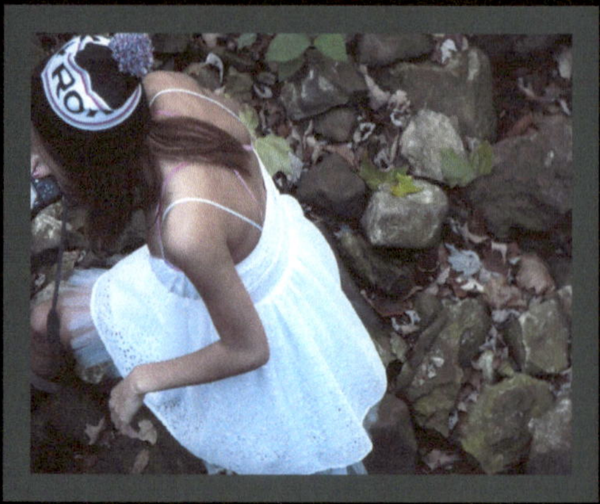

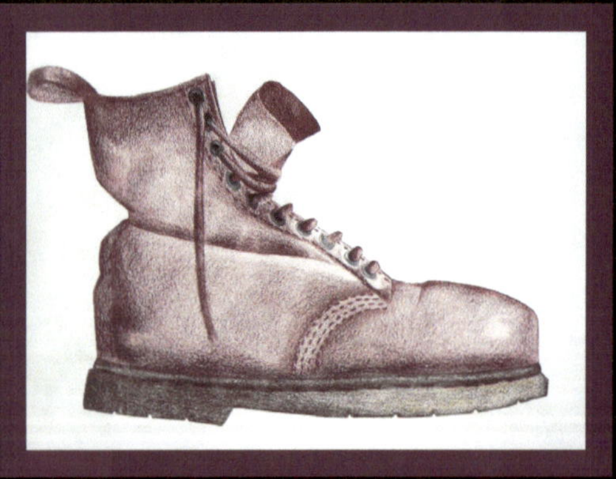

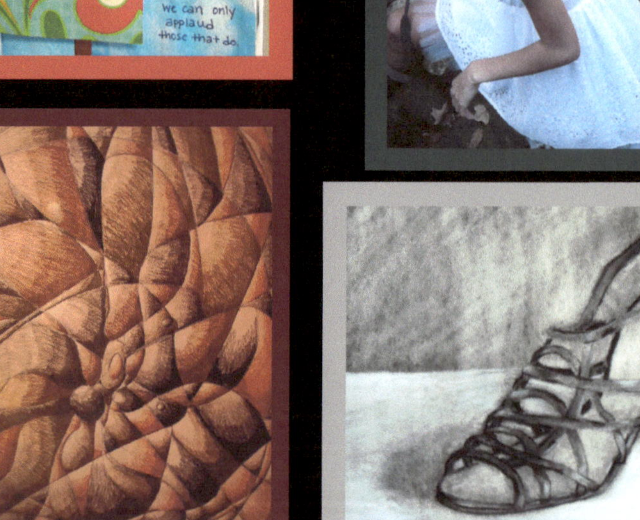

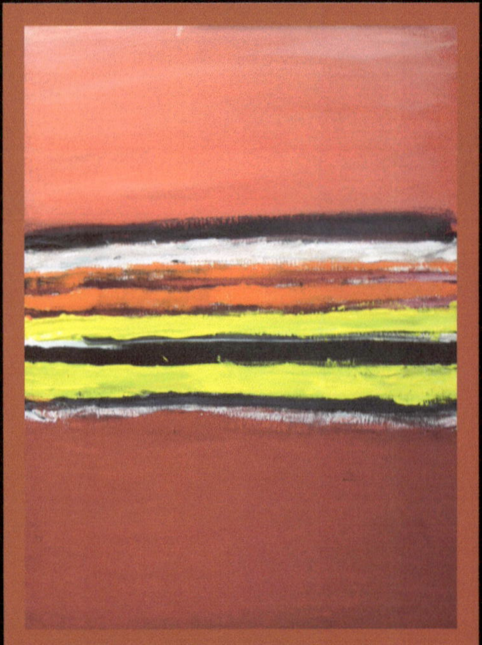

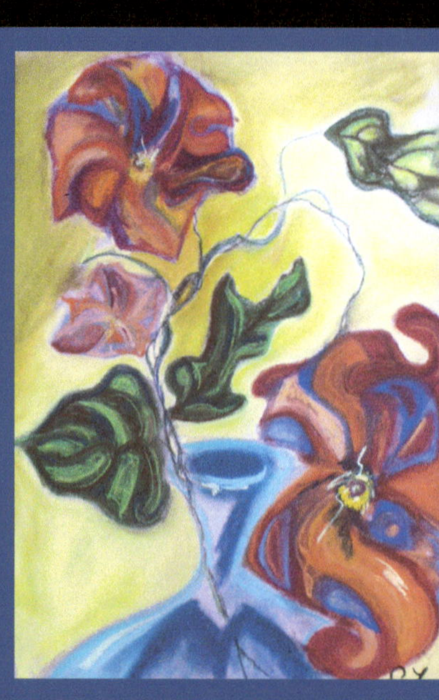

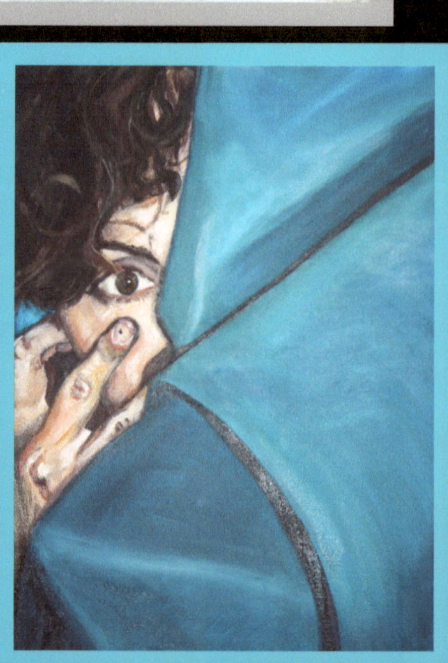

www.ingramcontent.com/pod-product-compliance
Lightning Source LLC
LaVergne TN
LVHW070140110826
845147LV00002B/294

9780578089652